3 ∞

embracing life again

Finding God Faithful in the Midst of Loss

Gwen Bagne

Foreword by Larry Burkett

WINEPRESS WP PUBLISHING

ISBN 1-57921-215-8
Library of Congress Catalog Card Number: 99-60726

ACKNOWLEDGMENTS

It is impossible to sufficiently thank all those who prayed, listened, and encouraged me when my heart was bleeding and I thought it would never stop. I owe much to those who told me I had something to say and should say it in a book. Let me mention just a few. . . .

Mom showed me the way through widowhood by her example of thriving not just surviving. Steve's parents, Quent and Bernice, modeled how Christianity works in the trenches.

Dave, Mike, and Richie gave me the shove I needed to begin writing.

Sally, Lee, Sherrie, and Marc gave hours of time and helped move the project along.

Rick, Darcy, Mary, and Emily reminded me of important events to add to the final draft.

And finally, thanks to my wonderful family at Northwest Foursquare Church, for modeling Christ's love in so many practical ways.

I could not have traveled through this extremely painful part of my life without the support of my family and those I refer to as "my people." I will forever be in your debt.

CONTENTS

FOREWORD

Gwen and Steve Bagne were an example of what God can do when we entrust our lives to him. Steve, with God's leading, and Gwen, with Steve's encouragement, turned their financial condition "about face," as they came to know that *He* could handle their finances far better than they could. This resulted in a change in *all* their circumstances, their lifestyle, and an increasing trust in the God of their salvation.

The same God who delivered them out of their financial bondage, once again proved himself faithful to them as they walked through the deep waters of Steve's illness, and his subsequent death. God sustained them, even through dark days. Steve continued to be an encouragement to Gwen, even though *all* their circumstances were once again changing.

The Psalmist says, "My flesh and my heart may fail; But God is the strength of my heart and my portion forever . . . as for me, the nearness of God is my good; I have made the Lord God my refuge, that I may tell of all Thy works" (73:26–28). In the past three years I have known Gwen, I have watched her proclaim all of God's works. I have watched her give glory to God for the life of her husband, praise God for leading them into financial freedom before they were faced with this trial of their lives, and thank God for using her, in spite of, as she candidly describes in *Embracing Life Again*, her doubts and fears.

I have no doubt God will continue to use Gwen through this book and through her ministry to widows as she comes alongside those who have walked her same path.

LARRY BURKETT
FOUNDER AND CEO
CHRISTIAN FINANCIAL CONCEPTS

INTRODUCTION

There are those who stand surefooted on the shores of life. My husband, Steve, was one of those individuals. He loved a challenge.

While camping in Oregon some years ago, he suggested we explore the lava caves. As we arrived in front of the underground chamber, my heart sank when I read the sign near the entry, "Do not disturb the bats." Standing beside Steve and looking into the blackness, I shivered in the chilly air. I stepped behind my husband and held the belt loops of his jeans. Burying my face into his back and walking on the heels of his shoes, we began the journey. Flashlight in hand, Steve confidently strode into the blackness. This was not my choice. I despised him for taking me in that horrible place.

Everything in me wanted to run out, but Steve encouraged me on. I trusted him and continued deeper into the cave. Each sound echoed in the eerie darkness, and my fear peaked when a drop of moisture touched my hair. A scream rose from within me as I imagined bat droppings on my head. Steve's calming voice reassured me it would be all right.

My eyes sought the sunlight as we turned to leave the cave. Stepping out, I breathed a sigh of relief. It was over. I didn't die, and it didn't last forever.

Little did I know that years later I would stand beside Steve facing another dark cave, the diagnosis of his terminal illness.

Embracing Life Again is a message of hope that reaches beyond surviving tragedy. God led me into sorrow, but he also brought me out. "God doesn't originate everything He permits, but He has determined to steer what He hates to accomplish what He loves" (*When God Weeps*, by Joni Eareckson Tada).

What does God love? First, he loves us and he loves to show himself faithful to bring us through the dark places of life. What does He achieve? That's my story.

✺ 1 ✺

STORM WARNINGS

Though the rain comes in torrents, the floods rise and the storm winds beat against his house, it won't collapse, for it's built on rock. Matthew 7:25

It was a chilly, sunny afternoon on January 18, 1993. As I sat in my car at the restaurant parking lot waiting for Steve, the noonday sun filtered through the car windows in a cascade of rainbows. I felt a heady sense of anticipation for the new year, for all Steve and I were planning.

I watched Steve's work van turn into the parking lot. I looked on as Steve parked, opened the door, and walked toward me. His 5-foot 10-inch, 150-pound frame looked trim and strong. At forty-five his auburn hair was still thick with just a slight hint of graying. Steve worked hard to keep in good physical shape, just as he worked hard to keep his mind and house in good order.

I marveled at the warmth and excitement I felt about this man—my best friend, my husband. I got out of the car to meet him, and we walked hand-in-hand into the local Red Robin restaurant.

The waitress directed us to a booth near a large window from where we could see a courtyard garden, dormant from the winter. After she took our order Steve began telling me how well his annual physical went that morning. His heart was strong, and his reflexes were good—he had passed with flying colors and was in great condition. I didn't expect anything less, but it was good to hear an expert confirm my own biased evaluation.

We talked about the coming year and all the promises it held, then we switched the conversation to our favorite topic, our biblical finances class. We wanted to increase our teaching ministry so we could help more people become better stewards of God's resources.

Lunch ended much too soon. Steve walked me to the car, kissed me good-bye, then went on to work. I drove home, so thankful for God's many blessings.

Talking about our future caused me to reflect on our not too distant past as I drove down Milton Way toward home. Steve and I are so different. My husband loved to have all his ducks in a row, kept perfect records, always balanced the checkbook, and was a saver. I, on the other hand, was impulsive, did not keep good records, and avoided balancing the checkbook. We were so different, but together we seemed to have found our way into a financial crisis just two years ago. I thought about how easy it was to purchase a home beyond our means and a recreational vehicle we couldn't afford and charge to the limit of our credit cards. It sounded like the American Dream when we started. Steve made a good salary, but it didn't seem to be enough for all of our living. As we began to look at what we were doing and where it was taking us, we realized we were actually living the American Nightmare. In too much debt and troubled about how we could let ourselves get into this fix, we knew we had to do something. We began to pray and ask God for help. One summer day when the pressure was really building, we decided to escape in our camper to the Oregon coast. That's when He answered us.

We stopped at a local bookstore to get reading material for the trip. Steve walked to the financial section, while I wandered to the light reading aisle for a novel. My husband came out with the book *Debt-Free Living* by Larry Burkett. This book was to lead us on a journey from bondage to freedom. Steve read Larry's book in less than three days. We spent the remaining four days of our vacation planning how we were going to turn our finances around.

Over the next two years we tracked our spending. Every evening we itemized our daily expenses even down to a latté. We soon realized we needed to sell our house. When the house sold six months later, we paid off the camper and credit card debt, moved into a rented townhouse, and continued to learn more about managing money God's way.

Our goal now was to get on a budget (living below our means), to get out of debt, and be able to give more into God's work. It wasn't long before we were teaching and counseling others with Larry Burkett's material. We discovered when God gives us something, like freedom from debt, it's always his plan for us to pass the good news on to others.

That same year on another camping trip, Steve purchased another book—Ron Blue's *Mastering Your Money*. Late into the night Steve read excerpts from a chapter on depreciation. The book explained the folly of investing in a depreciating asset when better investments can provide future income and independence. This challenged Steve to consider selling his much-loved depreciating camper—the one he washed, detailed, outfitted, and stored. After much discussion during our trip home, we agreed to put an advertisement in the paper. Within a few weeks the camper sold. With heavy hearts we unloaded all the gear from our little home on wheels.

We missed the camper, but we were completely out of debt and experiencing great freedom. We continued to teach others at church the good news of living debt-free. Fifteen months after moving into a rented townhouse, we purchased a home which we could pay off in five to seven years. A few months later we had saved enough in our recreation account to pay cash for a used camper. We were on the road again!

Pulling into the driveway after lunch that day, I sat amazed at God's work in our lives. Steve and I were happily married, our kids were raised, we were out of debt, and we were working together in a ministry we loved. Life looked great, abundant with God's blessings.

Three o'clock that same afternoon, Steve called and asked me to meet him at Seattle's Virginia Mason hospital. Dr. Rudolph told Steve to meet him there because tests revealed his blood count was alarmingly low.

I had an uneasy feeling as I backed out of the driveway and headed up I-5 toward Seattle. I met Steve in the lobby of the hospital. We joined hands without saying a word and walked into the elevator. When the door opened on the oncology wing, we walked toward the receptionist. Steve told her we had an appointment to see Dr. Rudolph. She directed us to room 102.

The room was dimly lit, giving it an almost surreal feeling. We sat in two chairs by the magazine rack. Leaning next to Steve, my arm around the back of his chair, we waited in silence.

Dr. Rudolph arrived about ten minutes later. After introducing himself, he told us he was concerned about Steve's low blood count.

Interrupting him, I asked, "Could this be a big nothing?"

"No," he answered, "this is definitely something."

We were stunned. We both felt numb and incredulous as Dr. Rudolph talked about what the numbers might mean—*cancer*. It was as if the doctor was talking to someone else and we were just listening. Dr. Rudolph had already scheduled a bone marrow biopsy before we arrived. Steve wanted me to stay while the doctor performed the procedure.

Still numb from hearing the words "biopsy" and "cancer," I watched my husband remove his jeans and lay face down on the examination table. Dr. Rudolph made a small puncture through the skin and into the hipbone to remove some bone marrow. He said we wouldn't know the results for three days.

We walked silently down the hall to the elevators then out of the hospital to our cars. We were surprised to see a dark parking lot and feel the rush of cold wind from what would become known as the Inauguration Day Storm. Cold and numb, we fought the wind and walked toward our vehicles. Before he opened my car door, Steve put his arms around me and held me close. Following my leader and my friend, I pulled my car behind his into the darkened street for the drive home.

✒ LIVING MATTERS ✑

- Oswald Chambers said, "We imagine we would be all right if a big crisis arose; but the big crisis will only reveal the stuff we are made of—crises always reveal character."

- A mentor of mine once told me, "Gwen, decide now that you will never deny your faith, that no matter what comes you will always follow God's path." I confidently stated that I would always stay the course. I believe we will all be faced with an opportunity to choose God in a dark moment.
- What kind of a crisis or storm would challenge the decisions you have made in life? Job loss? Divorce? Death of a loved one? Poor health? Financial collapse?

❧ 2 ❧

STORMY WEATHER

*The Lord is the light of my salvation-whom shall I fear?
The Lord is the stronghold of my life-of whom shall I be
afraid?* Psalm 27:1

The road home was long, dark, and treacherous. The
raging storm knocked down trees, destroyed roofs,
and took down power lines. As I followed closely
behind Steve, struggling to keep his work van in view, I
marveled at how secure I felt with this man God gave me—
even along a dark, precarious road. How different life had
once been. Before I knew Steve, the people in my life weren't
always dependable.

I remember waking up the morning of August 22, 1976,
thinking about my life. *I'm twenty-seven years old, divorced,
with two little boys to raise, working at a job I hate and trying
to fill the emptiness with another lousy relationship. I live on
the edge, constantly waiting for the other shoe to drop. What
am I going to do?*

I was raised in an alcoholic home with little security. I knew my father loved me when he was sober. But his many absences and our numerous moves to support his Army career added to the insecurity I felt during his frequent drinking sprees. Mom provided a semblance of stability and hope, but even she felt moments of desperation. My three brothers, three sisters, and I were always waiting for the volcano to erupt—we never knew what might happen next.

At the vulnerable age of fifteen, seeking love and security, I escaped into a relationship with a young man. This led to a pregnancy at seventeen and a marriage for which we were ill-equipped. Later, drugs, alcohol, and unfaithfulness on the parts of both of us brought our nine-year marriage to an end and I attempted to escape through divorce.

I continued to follow the destructive cycle of my youth, with all its uncertainties and dead-end streets. When life became too unbearable, I tried once again to retreat in a bottle, drugs, taverns, and in promiscuity. Feeling helpless and empty, I wondered if there was a better way to live. Was it possible my brother Jack had really discovered the way?

Jack had found Christianity four years earlier. He sent letters to the whole family telling of a Savior named Jesus Christ and how God had given him peace and purpose. To me Jack wrote, "Gweny, you need to get out of the taverns and give your life to the Lord."

Eventually Jack would lead our whole family out of darkness into the light. Within a year Mom gave her life to Christ. Over the next five years, five of the seven children in our family became Christians. I wanted what my brother and my mom had. On that August morning in 1976, it was time to stop running in the dark and step into the light. I called mom and said, "I'm going to church today to get saved." There was silence at the other end. I knew she was crying. God had heard and answered the prayers of a mom.

I arrived at Faith Tabernacle Church at ten o'clock that morning. I didn't have a deep understanding of the Bible, but I knew that Jack walked down an aisle at church to give his life to Jesus and I wanted to do the same. I don't recall anything the preacher said that morning, but when he asked for those who wanted to meet Jesus Christ to come forward, I did not hesitate. A young woman shared the gospel message with me. She told me Romans 10:9–10 says, "If you will acknowledge and confess with your lips that Jesus is the Lord and in your heart believe that God raised Jesus from the dead, you will be saved." She went on, "The Bible says that with our heart we believe and with our mouth we confess and confirm our salvation. Do you understand? Gwen, is this what you want to do?"

I answered firmly, "Yes!"

She then led me through a prayer of commitment, and on that morning in August, I gave my heart and my life to Jesus Christ. Leaving the church altar that day, I never looked back to my old, empty life.

With God's Word and his people to help me, I found freedom from the destruction of drugs, alcohol, and promiscuity. It wasn't easy, but I gained tools for living, and my children, Danny and Jake, had a whole new mother.

Two years later, Steve and I met at a singles' retreat. Friends from the start, we spent the next year and a half getting to know each other.

I learned Steve was raised in a Christian home with one brother and sister. But at fifteen he walked away from the God of his youth, thinking he could depend on himself to get by. At twenty, Steve married someone who also depended on herself and on earthly pleasures rather than on God.

Steve's salary as an electrician and his wife's income enabled them to enjoy many material comforts and "toys," but they were not prepared to deal with each other or the emptiness of a life without God.

After seven years Steve's marriage ended in divorce. And while he still had his boat, cars, truck, and many other luxuries, Steve felt empty and unfulfilled. Then one day in April, two years after Steve's divorce, a co-worker shared his faith, reminding Steve how secure he had once felt with God. Those thoughts stayed with Steve throughout the week. As was his habit, Steve decided he would escape to the solitude of his boat and think things through. Relaxing in the middle of Lake Washington that beautiful April day, Steve began to reflect on his life. He had all the material things the world could offer, yet he was empty. He thought, *I'm thirty. I have no wife, no family. I can never get on with my life until I give it back to God.* Suddenly, Steve turned his boat around and headed back to the dock. Running to his truck, he drove home, showered, threw on some clothes, and started for the church his friend attended.

Pulling into the church parking lot, Steve rushed through the doors just in time to see Roy Johnson step onto the platform. Steve recognized him as an evangelist who had visited the church he was raised in. Reverend Johnson seemed to speak directly to him, but when the call for a commitment came, Steve got up and walked out. As he began the drive home, he heard in his heart, *"This is your last opportunity!"*

Making a U-turn, Steve drove back to the church. Although the service was over, Steve found someone in the hallway. The man asked, "What can I do for you?" Steve, unable to speak, began to weep. The man took Steve to the pastor's office. On April 9, 1978, Steve began his journey back to God.

Steve touched me with his compassion and sincerity, and he helped me in my own journey as a Christian. He was my first male friend who did not seem to have an ulterior motive. In our friendship we discussed God's ways of handling finances, children, relationships, and our own personal growth in Christ.

God used Steve often to challenge me in many areas. On one occasion when I desperately wanted to attend a Bible study and was unable to find a babysitter, he dared to say, "Gwen, maybe you need to stay home with your kids tonight." On another occasion when I shared with Steve that I couldn't afford to tithe, he told me boldly but gently to step out and trust God and see what would happen. Steve was correct, and God continued to meet my needs as I tithed.

Remembering these conversations makes me smile because they were typical in our friendship. Steve always spoke the truth in love, and the direction from him was continually given in kindness, never condemning. God was impacting me through this unique relationship from the start. Steve became a trustworthy friend, someone I could depend upon. We fell in friendship long before we fell in love.

In 1980, when our friendship had grown into committed love, we married. My marriage to Steve brought a time of healing and learning to trust in new ways. For the first time in my life, I could take a deep breath, knowing what it meant to count on someone in every way. My sons grew to love and respect Steve. In turn, Steve gave them love, a wonderful knowledge of God, and a stability so lacking in their lives. God gave me exceedingly, abundantly above what I had asked. We serve a God of second chances, who takes broken hearts and lives and redeems them.

How easy it was to let Steve, my friend, lead me. For twelve years I followed him. There he was, right in front of me as usual, gently leading me home. I said quietly to the Lord, "I am so grateful; life is so safe and secure. I love Steve so much."

As we drove into the driveway, there were no lights anywhere. The large cedar trees around our home swayed like never before, leaving large branches all over the yard. Without power our house was cold and pitch-dark.

I found the candles while Steve started a fire in the woodstove. In silence we wrapped a blanket around us, cuddled up on the couch, watched the fire, and listened to the raging storm. Breaking the silence, Steve asked, "What are you most afraid of?"

Heart pounding, I said, "That you'll die and I'll be left to live without you." Then I asked him, "What are you most afraid of?"

"That I'll die and you'll be left alone."

We held each other and tried to pray, but mostly we cried.

The storm raged throughout the night, and when we awoke the next morning, the yard was covered with branches from our cedar trees. Looking out at the debris, I sensed another even more devastating kind of storm was about to blow into our lives.

✍ LIVING MATTERS ✌

- Corrie ten Boom said, "God's love still stands when all else has fallen."
- There was a time when answers for life were on the tip of my tongue. I had formulas that held me up and I could run to my husband,

my friend, when my life turned upside down.
These blueprints for life were a safety net and
refuge in the past storms of my life.

- Who or what is your safe-place, and who is
your resource in the dark times? (Husband?
Money? Children? Friends? Church?)

❦ 3 ❧

Something Strange

Do not be surprised at the painful trial you are suffering, as though something strange were happening to you. But rejoice. 1 Peter 4:12

Three days finally passed. Dr. Rudolph entered his office at Virginia Mason Hospital where Steve and I were waiting to hear his verdict. We sat close together with fingers intertwined. You could see the whites of our knuckles, holding on to life with all the strength we could muster. As the doctor sat down behind his desk and moved his chair toward us, we were afraid to breathe—afraid, yet at the same time anxious to hear his words.

Dr. Rudolph barely mumbled a greeting before the words "leukemia," "bone marrow transplant," and "donor search" began tumbling out of his mouth. Our minds were racing, trying to grasp what he was saying. My heart pounded as I sat there, angry with the doctor. Obviously, he had spoken these words many times. We were just one of the many to whom he had pronounced a death sentence. Our only hope was to find a bone marrow donor, and even if we found the donor, the odds were still not good.

Well! I was not about to accept Dr. Rudolph's diagnosis. No way! Doctors don't have all the answers and, after all, we had God! Maybe they had merely made a mistake. I just knew God was going to make everything okay so we could get back to our lives and the real purpose God had for us, according to my definition of "real purpose." God's people would pray, the pastor would anoint Steve with oil, and God would heal him—simple as that! Surely this was just some kind of a test we had to pass. We tithed and followed the rules God had laid out for us. Surely our Savior would rescue and shelter us from this attack.

On January 22, 1993, Steve began writing in his journal. As was so typical, Steve analyzed the circumstances surrounding his illness, looking to find God's direction and purpose for his life and even his possible death. "[I'm] very blessed with a beautiful wife, wonderful family, in-laws, house, job, budget, and health. Now, with a bump in the road threatening loss, I find my life and eyes have been on these [earthly things]."

Steve went to work the next day. Outwardly he was the same, strong Steve, but his journal revealed his struggle: "[I'm] starting to feel pressure. [I] went to work and faked it—not sure what to say. [In the] evening we began to share with a few good friends from church. [I'm] still trying to stay up [in spirits], but tears [are] beginning to come."

I remained in denial, refusing to believe I could lose my husband. Reality began to set in as weekly hospital visits stretched into months and I watched Steve steadily lose strength.

A bone marrow search was being made through Fred Hutchinson Cancer Center in Seattle. This began within the immediate family, because a match, even if not perfect, is preferable. If family members were ruled out, it would become necessary to go to the registry. There was much anxiety, as we waited for the news. When we finally heard that Steve's parents, brother, sister, and nephews were not considered even a slight possibility, the fear intensified.

Emily, Steve's sister, was especially angry with God, when she and her brother Jim turned out not to be a match. "Here we are," she said tearfully. "It would seem the most logical and expedient way for God to work!"

The next step was to take Steve's blood, process it, and give the results to the American Registry and the National Marrow Donor Program. The likelihood of finding a matched unrelated donor depends on a number of factors. The first is the patient's haplotypes—the set of six HLA antigens inherited from your parents. These six numbers are like a fingerprint. If these haplotypes are fairly common, the chances of finding a matched donor in the current National Marrow Donor Program registry of 600,000 donors is quite good. Patients with very rare haplotypes, on the other hand, have less then a 10 percent chance of finding a donor. Steve, we soon discovered, would fall into the rare group. Locating a donor would take the work of God alone.

Many friends went to the local blood bank to be tested and processed as a potential bone marrow match. Even Steve's employer, MacDonald-Miller Company, did a blood drive at work. We discovered how many were searching and waiting for a donor and the importance of having a large pool from which to select. There was a need especially for more minorities. We were soon informing everyone to contact The

National Marrow Donor Program at 800-654-1247 to find out how to become a bone marrow donor.

As the months passed, Steve became weaker and could no longer protect me from the world and tell me everything would be all right. I had to fight my battles alone because Steve was facing his own war. Security and safety in my life and in Steve eroded. As Steve became less the man I could rely upon, I, too, was becoming less and less myself. I wanted to call a time-out. This was not supposed to happen. As Steve's wife I was taken care of—a kept woman.

I did not like the change in our roles. My mind screamed, *Oh God, how I hate this!* Rage began to creep into my heart. One evening the anger spilled out. Through clenched teeth, I asked, "Why us? Why now?"

Steve's response was, "Why not us? Who are we?"

Words of prayer and support began to come through family and friends. As Steve grew weaker, our church, Northwest Foursquare, and many others, surrounded us with help in very practical ways. I particularly remember the evening a friend came to fix a leaky faucet and Steve, who was always the giver, was now the receiver. It was difficult for Steve and me to receive and even more difficult for Steve to progressively lose control over the common everyday details of his life.

Chaplain Tom spoke wise words when he said, "We think we can control so much in life, but control is an illusion." He was right. But giving up the misconception of control is not easy. As friends and loved ones challenged us to take the hands that were being extended, we learned to lean on God and others and to let go of the we-can-do-it-ourselves attitude. By listening and learning, we discovered new things about God's people and ourselves.

There were other words spoken by kind but unthinking people. Condemning statements were given with such confidence to my sweet husband, who was so desperately struggling just to stay alive. "You should read this book," they said. "You should tithe. . . . You should use your electrician skills to help others. . . . You should repent for teaching about money management instead of about Jesus." Though well meaning, these people did not understand we had already examined anything and everything we could, and we had already promised to change in any way God wanted us to if only he would heal Steve.

God used us to teach biblical principles for managing money so we could help others, and we had been able to help many find financial freedom by following God's money management plan. We knew without a doubt that because we had followed biblical standards, we were in a secure financial position, even as we faced this health crisis.

Words from ignorant people had a devastating effect on two very fragile people. But we chose to consider the source and let go of condemning comments. We had to conserve all our energy for the right battles. When we shared the unkind remarks with our pastor, Steve Schell, he said, "These kind of people are what I like to refer to as, 'Santa's Helpers.' That's about how real they are."

While the donor search proceeded, which had eliminated all family members, we began seeking alternative methods of healing: naturopathic doctors, vitamins, minerals, juicing, barley greens, and exercise, all of which helped Steve's energy, but did not touch the bone marrow. We did all we could, even begging and bargaining with God to give us our lives back.

Steve told me one afternoon, "Even if God healed me tomorrow, we will never be who we used to be, this has changed us." Once again I realized I did not feel at home. This journey was something strange.

✌ LIVING MATTERS ✌

- Oswald Chambers said, "Has God trusted you with silence—a silence that is big with meaning? God's silences are His answers."
- When all that could be done had been done and heaven was like brass, God seemed cruel, and despair overcame me. His truth is higher than what was happening, and God's Word was not silent in my soul. It reminded me that I was not alone.
- Has there been a time when you did not get the answer you wanted and there was only silence? How did you respond?

✍ 4 ✍

SEARCHING FOR LIFE

I have searched for you with all my heart; be gracious to me according to your promise. Psalm 119:58

Four months passed without finding a bone marrow donor. My fear increased each week as Steve's strength decreased. Where was God in all of this? Why didn't he save Steve? My husband was dying before my eyes.

The Fred Hutchinson Cancer Research Center was searching for a donor in the International Bone Marrow Transplant Registry while at the same time Steve's bone marrow was shutting down. His system wasn't producing enough red cells to carry oxygen throughout his body, robbing him of energy. Yet Steve valiantly continued to go through each day, trying to maintain a normal schedule at work.

In March 1993, we realized we could no longer keep pace with life as it had been. It was painful to finally consider giving up our financial teaching ministry. Sharing with others had brought much joy into our lives, and I was resentful and angry with God for allowing this disease to come in and rob us in this way.

In April, Steve could no longer work and was placed on disability pay. God had prepared us two years earlier for living on 60 percent of our income. Our standard of living was not affected when Steve went on disability. Though this was half of his salary, we were still able to pay all our bills and, yes, even save. *Had God directed us, knowing we would be facing this crisis?*

Just before Memorial Day weekend 1993, Steve went to the dentist for a checkup. When the doctor began working in Steve's mouth, his gums started to bleed. Unable to stop the bleeding, the dentist sent us to the emergency room.

The doctor on call decided to admit Steve into the hospital because his platelet count was extremely low, indicating the leukemia was advancing. When the lifesaving replacement platelets finally arrived at midnight, Steve's gums were still bleeding. My husband told me to go home and said he would call in the morning. I left with a heavy heart. It was our first separation, just one of many to come, and our faith was challenged anew.

When I arrived at the hospital room the next day, Steve described how, late into the night, as he watched the platelets drip through the IV line into his arm, he asked God, "Why are you using another man's platelets when you could stop the bleeding with your little finger?" Steve went on to say, "The presence of peace entered the room, and I fell asleep. When I awoke, someone on the television was singing about Jesus, and I began to weep. The platelets had finished dripping in, and my gums weren't bleeding. In my heart I heard the words, 'I gave my Son on the cross. I don't have to prove myself. I have already done enough.'

"Gwen," Steve spoke firmly, "I want to be healed, but if God doesn't do another thing for me, He's already done enough. He has given His Son!"

Looking back, I can see that Steve was still leading me to safe places. At the time I was stunned and frightened by his words; I felt he was giving up. Even though I somehow knew in my subconscious that he was speaking truth, it was difficult to let go. In my mind God still needed to heal my husband before I could say, "God, you have done enough."

Steve became dependent on transfusions to fight the cancer growing inside him. Each week we spent many hours in the hospital transfusion rooms. When Steve's blood count was low, he would receive a transfusion. When they were in the safe zone, we would go home. My emotions would rise and fall with his blood counts.

On one of these visits, when the nurse told us his counts were low, anger overwhelmed me. I stormed off the elevator.

Steve ran up behind me, took my hand, and sat me down. "Hey, where are you going? What is going on?"

"Listen," I said. "Either God is too busy to fix you or He's too tiny to fix you. So from now on I'm calling him 'Tiny.'"

Steve looked at me and said, "Gwen, God knows exactly where we are. This has not caught Him off guard. There is no panic in heaven, only plans. He is right here with us."

I cried in frustration, wondering where our miracle was, so we could get on with real life.

When we returned home that afternoon, we found a letter from our son Jake lying on Steve's pillow. It read:

Dad,

Hey Dad, long time no see huh? Yo, Jake is still around here sometimes. Well, I just wanted to tell you that I love you very much and to keep lookin' up. Mom said today was a bit of a letdown. But we have a secret weapon, prayer! I'm still prayin' and you better be as well [I'm sure you are]. Everyone I know is prayin' and pullin' for ya.

Just so you know, Danny and I, on Sunday, will be taking stuff in the backyard to the dump. I got my taxes done, and everything else is fine. So hang in there, Dad, and "everything and all that stuff . . . "

Love, your son

Steve and I smiled when we read Jake's letter. I knew Jake and Danny felt as helpless and confused as I did. They were trying to do everything they could to support us in our fight, like cleaning the backyard and giving us words of support. I felt so blessed to have a wonderful, supportive family. It meant so much.

I still refused to accept that Steve's leukemia was part of God's plan. I was not going to give up, even if Steve seemed to be. I began searching for a cure and asking the doctor a lot of questions. Each week I would come with magazine articles about new treatments for cancers. I would ask Dr. Rudolph, "What about this? Have you heard about this treatment?" He patiently answered each and every question, but Steve became very troubled because I was still clawing to find the answer to this "big mistake."

One afternoon, while we were having lunch in the hospital cafeteria, Steve said, "Gwen, please stop asking the doctor questions. You're not helping me. I don't want to know more than I need to know."

"This is how I'm coping!"

"You're not helping me, Gwen. I need you on my side."

I felt a jolt throughout my body, and I looked at Steve anew. I still had a lot of growing up to do. Steve was fighting for his life, while I was immaturely trying to gain solutions. Realizing I had to accept where we were and stop demanding things from God, I shifted my focus to supporting Steve and giving what he needed. But it wasn't easy.

More of the household duties were transferred into my charge. My anxiety increased with the added responsibility for the budget, bills, and balancing the checkbook. These were Steve's favorite jobs, but I was terrified. I fought the process. So each night when we were home, Steve patiently led me to the dining room table for our nightly training sessions.

As our nights at home became fewer, Steve placed into his briefcase all the information we would need—names, papers, phone numbers, policies, budget information, envelopes, stamps, and a calculator. It went everywhere we went so Steve could instruct me wherever we were. We would sit together, open the briefcase, and my husband and friend would gently talk me through the process of bill paying and recording each transaction. Later, this briefcase would become the tool that was mine—a security.

While I would later view this as an act of love, having to take Steve's role in the financial area was a struggle for me. I wanted so badly for there to be another way, because although he enjoyed all of it, I enjoyed none of it! Couldn't someone else do this for me? I was still looking for a way out.

There were many things I didn't want. I didn't want to take over the money management and reconciling the checkbook. I didn't want Steve to suffer through a bone marrow transplant. I didn't want to live without my husband.

I wanted my husband healed the quick way through God's miracle at the church altar with the anointing oil. God had always fit so neatly into my shiny, gift wrapped view of Him. I did not recognize Him any more. He was like a stranger to me. God was making me walk in the dark, and I didn't like it. I was looking for the light, looking for my healthy husband to be restored to me so that would vindicate the God I thought I knew.

As Steve's health continued to decline, we began asking, "What if they don't find a donor?" Nights were becoming more difficult. Steve was getting frequent nosebleeds and was up and down throughout the night.

One night, after moving into the guest room to sleep, I began to weep with such a sadness in my soul. The door opened, and Steve came in and crawled under the covers with me. He pulled me to him and just held me. I told him how much I missed him, how much I missed us. We fell asleep in each other's arms. I felt like God was hidden where I could no longer find Him. Nothing was clear, and life seemed to be a murky shadow.

As always, even in his weakness, Steve's faith was strong. After an especially trying week at the hospital, we came home and attended church Sunday morning. After church, Steve wrote in his journal:

> Got up early [this morning] to pray after being distracted all week. Went to church. The presence of the Holy Spirit [was] so strong that Gwen and I could hardly sing—the tears flowed.
>
> Pastor Steve called Gwen and me up front for prayer—overwhelming. [There were] several words of encouragement, [I was] anointed with oil and [Pastor Steve devoted] a long time [for] prayer. [The] support of God's people [was] amazing, [a] wonderful message on active faith.
>
> [Gwen and I] went home and reflected on the most wonderful Sunday we have had. Jesus is so great and loving and many people believed for God's healing.

✒ LIVING MATTERS ✑

- Wayne Watson sings, "I'd rather walk in the dark with Jesus, than to walk in the light on my own."
- As a little girl, I would sometimes wake in the middle of the night. Heart pounding, I searched for the door. Straining to see through the darkness, I felt along the walls for the way out so I could go to my parents' room. Though it seemed I would never find the door, eventually there it would be, a way out. Jesus is the only door in the dark that leads to the light.

✺ 5 ✺

SEEKING THE SAVIOR

*Without faith it is impossible to please God, because any-
one who comes to him must believe that he exists and that
he rewards those who earnestly seek him.* Hebrews 11:6

By the end of May, our lives revolved around Steve's
strength or the lack of it. He did have some weeks
that were better than others—weeks he felt *healthy.*
At one of those better times, the doctor gave us permission
to take a few days in our newly acquired camper. We left on
a Monday morning for Canon Beach, a favorite spot on the
Oregon coast. Fred Hutchinson Cancer Center gave us in-
structions to call about two o'clock that afternoon to check
on the donor search. All our family and friends were tested
and eliminated as possibilities. There were now three potential donors in the National and International marrow
pool left to process. Two of these donors were from England, and one had been ruled out that week.

Stopping at a gas station, Steve went to a phone booth and called Fred Hutchinson. I watched my husband from the cab of the truck. He hung up the receiver and returned to the camper. With no expression on his face, he slid behind the wheel. Quietly he said, "They ruled out the second donor from England. They'll know about number three in another week."

Oh, God, I thought, *What is going to happen?* We drove in silence to the RV site and set up camp.

The next two evenings were chilly, but Steve enjoyed the getaway. One night as we got ready to take one of our after-dinner walks, Steve announced he had a fever and didn't want to go out. He said, "Sweetie pie, you go ahead." With heaviness in my heart, I walked the beach alone.

The next day Steve felt a little better, and we ventured out toward the ocean. As he headed down the trail to the beach, I lingered behind, snapping a picture of him as he walked away from me toward the water. It was a sad moment knowing this would be our last trip for a long time. Later we broke camp and left on the four-hour drive home.

The afternoon we got home, Steve was admitted to the hospital for another transfusion and I was scrubbing the camper floor. Sorrow welled up in my heart. *Please, Jesus,* I pleaded, *I need to see you. I can't see your face because fear is blocking my view. Please take the fear away and be with me. If you will come with me, I can go through anything that's ahead.*

It had been a long time since I asked God simply for His presence. As I called out to the God I said I trusted, I felt His powerful presence and peace come into my anxious soul. Oswald Chambers says, "His blessings are nothing in comparison to Himself."

I quit praying for the donor of the bone marrow and began searching for the God who made the bone marrow. One hour later, the Fred Hutchinson donor coordinator called to tell us the third donor was a match. A perfect six antigen match with the same rare haplotypes. We beat the 10 percent odds of finding a donor. Even the coordinator said it was a miracle. The donor's HLA numbers were identical to Steve's. God had a plan the whole time.

Was this the beginning of our new life? Excitement filled my heart. Finding a donor, the thing I opposed six months ago, now caused my heart to rejoice.

Even though I knew the painful process would take one hundred days, we had already beat the odds. It seemed now to be our only chance. I immediately called the hospital. The operator put me through to Steve. When he answered, I almost whispered with hesitant anticipation, "Steve, Fred Hutchinson called. They found a donor."

There was silence on the other end of the phone. Steve was overcome with emotion. "Steve," I continued, "do you think this is the Lord?"

Steve spoke tearfully, "We have to make up our minds, Gwen; either we are in God's hands, or we're not. I believe we are. This is the only door open to us, and we are going to go through it. Gwen, we aren't going to ask this question anymore. We are in God's hands."

Though Steve's words were gentle instruction, they fell on the skeptical ears of a reluctant student. Just then a verse of a song came to my mind—*The ship is battered but the anchor held; the sails are torn but the anchor held.* Would my anchor hold as this storm of a lifetime started to grow in intensity? Would my spiritual sails take me to safe harbor?

Father's Day, June 1993, we drove to the small coastal town of Ocean Shores to visit Steve's dad and mom. We wanted to spend time with his parents before entering the hospital for the bone marrow transplant. When we arrived, emotions were running high. Steve and his dad took time to walk and talk and grew closer during that visit.

When we returned home, the following Monday, two Father's Day cards from Danny and Jake were lying on the dining room table.

> Dearest Dad,
> Thanks for everything you've done for me in my life. I know you and I don't talk that much, because I always seem to talk to Mom. But anyway, I love you and I hope you had a good Father's Day at Ocean Shores.
> Your son, Danny

> Dad,
> I just wanted to say Happy Father's Day, late, since no one was home last weekend. I love you, Dad, but I had a hard time picking you a gift, so this is what I came up with. NO it's not the card. My gift to you is a son, a son that will soon carry your name. Yes, that would be me. Happy Father's Day!!!
> Love, Jacob

Steve's eyes filled with tears. He reached for me, and we held each other and cried over of the goodness of God. Just twelve years earlier, God took four lives—Steve, Gwen, Danny, and Jacob—knit them together, and built a family unit. Our family was a testimony of God's power. It was truly one of those "God moments."

Fred Hutchinson Cancer Research Center or the "Hutch," as it was nicknamed by the employees, gave us a list of apartments they recommended. The center administrators encouraged bone marrow patients to move close to the hospital to accomodate the daily visits and assist in transplant preparations.

Steve's dad and I began the tedious process of locating a suitable apartment. I was stunned as my father-in-law took out his checkbook and informed me that he would be covering this expense. I felt overwhelmed by this act of generosity and told him, "I don't know when we will be able to repay you." He responded firmly, "This is my son we're talking about!"

Steve's parents had already given us a gas card for the many miles we were driving and a phone card for all the long distance calls we had to make. There were no words to express our appreciation. We could have taken money out of our retirement plan and were willing to do so, but God had another way of providing. For the next four months Steve's dad made the twelve-hundred-dollar-a-month rent payments.

On July 24, 1993, Steve and I moved to our furnished, one-bedroom apartment four blocks from the Hutch. The next morning, the bright warmth of the sun filled the car as we headed for our temporary home. It was a beautiful day for a drive into Seattle, though we faced uncertainty. Pulling into the parking garage of the apartment building, we grabbed a few things out of the backseat of the car and walked into the elevator. As the doors opened on the fourth floor, I followed Steve down the hall. We entered our very small, but clean, and airy apartment. The view from our only window looked on a very large and old red brick church. It had been there long before all the buildings had pressed in around it. The tall steeple reached into the sky above the busy streets as if to say, "I am not leaving; I am here to stay!"

We soon discovered every day at noon and again at six o'clock in the evening, bells rang out loud with the strong melody of an old hymn. The first song we heard from the old red brick church was "Amazing Grace," reminding us that God was there in the middle of the chaos.

The small but adequate kitchen was well lit and cheerful. The first thing I did was make a pot of coffee. The smell of the coffee brewing gave me comfort as I unpacked the few groceries we brought.

The bedroom had twin beds, a nightstand, and a six-drawer dresser with a mirror on it. Excited and hopeful, we were ready for life in the city and a chance for healing.

The next day we visited the outpatient clinic. Steve began to endure many tests in preparation for admission. They examined his eyes, teeth, throat, stomach, liver, kidneys, bowels, lung capacity, and muscle reflexes, did a spinal tap, and another bone marrow biopsy. These tests would be repeated again after the transplant. The results would be compared.

In the morning we were sent to Swedish Hospital to have a small flexible tube called a catheter (sometimes called a *Hickman* or "central venous line") inserted into a large vein in Steve's chest just above his heart. This tube enabled the medical staff to administer all Steve's drugs, blood products, and liquid diet. Through this catheter, the hundreds of blood samples required during the course of the treatment were painlessly taken, without inserting needles into his arms or hands.

We had paperwork and protocol to get through while Steve was becoming weaker. Then something new started to happen. Steve began to suffer fevers daily, indicating white cells were frighteningly low. Fred Hutchinson tried to accelerate the process and admit him quickly. Finally, on August 1, the doctors told us to prepare for admission the next morning. The transplant process would take approximately one hundred days after entering the hospital. The night before admission to the hospital, we lay in one of the apartment's two single beds, talking into the night.

"Steve, can you believe we're here in this position?"

"We are in God's hands," he reminded me as he squeezed me tightly.

Not knowing what the future would bring, we held each other close, as though it were our last embrace. I fought the reality of the odds against us. Even with Steve's perfect donor match, he could die from a number of causes before the transplant was even completed.

Pressing my face into Steve's neck, I told him, "I wish we could go home. Can't we just go home?"

"I wish we could," he said, holding me firmly.

The fear of being separated was overwhelming. All of a sudden I just wanted to run away. I did not want to let him go into that place, afraid I would lose him, afraid that he might not come out. Keeping these thoughts to myself, I snuggled closer to Steve. I couldn't get close enough, but I felt as long as I could hold on to him, we were safe.

The next morning we walked to the hospital holding hands. The lovely, warm summer day seemed strange as we faced the unknown darkness ahead. We squeezed each other's hands in fearful anticipation as we walked into the center's reception area. I recalled an interview with a doctor two months earlier. The doctor had said, "Only 50 percent of those who enter the hospital survive." I gripped Steve's hand tightly as the lump in my throat became almost unbearable.

Knowing we had only a few hours before Steve would be admitted, we left the center and ate lunch in a sunny sidewalk café, after which we went for a walk and then headed back. Each step was filled with hope and fear.

We were pleased to see an oversized chair when we walked into Steve's hospital room, his new home for the next month. We sat together and held hands in the big chair while we waited. Behind the plastic curtain there was a bed waiting for its occupant. A television hung on the wall in the corner. There was a side table near the bed, a small closet, and an exercise bike pushed up against the window. Through the window, I could see men at work on a building under construction across the street. The world around us was completely unaware of our pending danger as we sat silently, huddled in the chair. The nurse came much too soon and told us it was time for Steve to walk across the threshold.

Crossing the threshold meant letting go of the hand of the only earthly man I had ever been able to completely rely upon. What was coming would change Steve and me forever. The ensuing treatments would cause Steve's immune system to evaporate, leaving him vulnerable to all kinds of illnesses. The thick plastic wall helped ward off fatal diseases. While Steve lived in that small room, we could see each other, but he could have no physical contact with anyone.

Tears in his eyes, Steve let go of my hand. I numbly watched as Steve went down the hall to a room where he would remove his street clothes and dress in the hospital gown the nurse gave him. When I saw Steve again, we could only look at each other. He walked across the forbidden line into the room with the thick plastic wall so he could begin the difficult road to a cure.

Standing in the hallway, I allowed tears to roll down my face as the many people around me went about their business. An ache began to creep through my body. I felt paralyzed, like a child who was lost, wondering which way to go. I felt so lonely—*God, I have never felt so alone.*

At our wedding, my brother Tom sang a song by Bob Cull, "Only the Beginning." One verse says, "When today is just a memory I want you to know, He'll still be working faithfully that your love in Him will grow. But it's only the beginning of a lifetime yet to come. Let your lives just be reflections of the one your love comes from." And this was another beginning of so much which lay ahead. The clear plastic wall hung like a cold steel shadow between us.

✌ LIVING MATTERS ✍

- It's said, "A faith that can't be tested can't be trusted." When our faith is challenged, this is when it finally finds its value. *Trust* literally means, "to have confidence in," and learning this is accomplished only through the testing of the belief.
- What if trusting God meant letting go of something you cherished?

✒ 6 ✑

SEPARATION

I am convinced that nothing can ever separate us from his love. Death can't, and life can't. Nothing will ever separate us from the love of God. Romans 8:38-39

Leaning against the wall, I watched as the nursing staff settled Steve into his new home. Trying to cheer myself up, my mind said, *I'm separated from my husband, but not from God.* But I could feel an ache beginning to rise up my chest.

A floor supervisor walked toward me, interrupting my thoughts. She asked, "How are you doing?"

A cry came out of my throat, and I burst into tears.

She put her arm around me, led me to a conference room, sat me down and spoke firmly. "Steve did not take out a lease on that room. People walk out of this place all the time."

It was as if God was speaking to me, as if He and I were having a conversation. It gave me a sense of peace.

There was a knock on the door. A woman leaned in and said, "Mrs. Bagne, there is a call for you."

The phone call was from Mike, a friend and co-worker of Steve's. He said, "Gwen, don't try to do this alone." Through people, God was letting me know that He was with me. God was not leaving me comfortless.

I began walking back to the apartment without Steve. It was strange and unnatural. As I entered the living room and sat alone on the couch, the church bells began to ring out their evening tune, "Because He lives, I can face tomorrow." Getting my journal, I wrote: "Moving into the unknown. Separation-alone-scared-anxious. God, Steve is in the Hutch! I am here on Spring Street. I'm so tired. Mike said not to try and do this alone."

The next morning Steve began receiving massive doses of chemotherapy. Initially feeling great, Steve ordered a large nonbacterial breakfast of eggs, sausage, and hash browns. But by noon he was vomiting hourly. This treatment continued until he received levels a human could barely endure without dying.

On the third day, Steve began total body radiation to remove all his bone marrow, a process that would destroy his immune system and every bit of hair on his body. Panic and anxiety were creeping into my heart. I steadied myself by thinking, *The nurses assigned to Steve's care are alert. They know this is a critical time, and they will watch over my husband.*

A nurse entered Steve's room. She helped him dress from head to foot with hood, facemask, gown, gloves, and booties. He looked like a character for a science fiction movie. Only his eyes were showing as he leaned against the nurse while she helped him into a wheelchair. The nurse wheeled Steve from behind the plastic sheet. I followed as she pushed his chair down a long narrow hallway, through metal doors, and into a large room.

The walls were pale teal with a wide, checked, red-and-white stripe around the center. In the middle was a metal table with a gray mattress. On the walls hung the large black radiation machines. Steve, weakened by two days of chemotherapy, struggled to lift himself out of the wheelchair and up onto the table. He lay quietly as the attendant strapped him down. She motioned for me to leave, and followed me out, leaving Steve in the room alone. My heart beat against my ribs as she pushed the metal doors closed and directed me toward a black and white television screen outside the radiation room. My eyes were glued to the viewing screen.

I vaguely heard her say, "Okay, we're about to begin." A buzzing sound began as she turned on the machine.

Steve lay motionless while the radiation destroyed his bone marrow and weakened him even more. He underwent this process five times in two days.

I admired my husband so much as I watched him face the days with quiet courage, diligently doing what was necessary even while the radiation took its toll. Steve became weak, irritable, and nauseous. He developed painful mouth sores as well. We had been forewarned, but it was still hard to watch as my husband endured the seemingly endless torture.

Each day Steve would rise early as the nurse pushed sterile water into his room through an opening in the plastic. He washed himself from the top of his now bald head to the soles of his feet. Because he was so weak and sick, Steve took many breaks while bathing. After dressing Steve rinsed his mouth with an antibacterial solution. With no immune system, bacteria caused his mouth to break out with sores. As the days passed, rinsing became very painful.

After Steve finished, he pushed the bath water, mouth solution, towels, and used hospital gowns out through the opening in the plastic. Then he took his pills and applied an ointment over his body. Afterward Steve fell into bed exhausted.

I would ask, "How are you doing in there?"

He would say, "I'm just trying to live. . . . I'm just trying to live."

A nurse examined Steve twice a day. Before entering the protective room, the nurse covered herself with a sterile gown, gloves, booties, and mask. A cleaning person entered Steve's room daily, covering him or herself in the same manner. Then the cleaning person washed everything in the room with an antibacterial solution, including the walls and plastic curtain. Everyone worked hard to keep bacteria from attacking my defenseless husband.

I rose early each morning in the small apartment I now shared with Steve's parents and my mother. I could see it was a heart-wrenching time for Steve's parents and my mom. Steve was the firstborn, and he had a very close relationship with his parents. Steve's dad was often overcome with emotion as he watched his son struggle through each day. And it was difficult for his mother to sit and look helplessly through the plastic wall separating her from her son. My mom adored her son-in-law and referred to him as her son. Since mom's widowhood, she had come to rely upon Steve. They had a special bond.

Each morning I dressed, ate breakfast, and walked to the Hutch. After receiving updates about Steve's progress, I would receive and return calls, send cards, and greet visitors at the elevator. Daily I passed on news about Steve's progress to those who were walking with us through this difficult time. My mom and Steve's parents would come in shifts so someone was with Steve at all times.

I wore a pager a friend gave me so I could leave for short breaks, knowing the hospital could reach me at all times. At times the pager would beep, and I'd look to see what number to call. There would be four 7s on the small screen. This was a code from Rick and Darcy that at that very moment they were praying. It always lifted my spirit, knowing someone was thinking about and praying for us as we faced the daily hurdles.

During the first four days Steve was in the sterile room, I became acquainted with other families and we began bonding. In a room near the reception area there were couches, overstuffed chairs, a television, toys for small children, and a pot of coffee. Family members of other patients congregated here throughout the day. This was a place to stop and share our lives now connected by cancer. As we talked and listened to each other's stories, those who were there longer told the rest what to expect.

I met Linda, whose husband, Dave, was also a leukemia patient. Linda and Dave Bordonaro were from Connecticut and were Christians. Dave had suffered with leukemia for eight years before finding a donor in Italy. Linda and I shared our stories about our husbands.

Dave's room was three doors down the hall from Steve. Since Dave had begun his bone marrow transplant nine days before Steve, he had regained a little strength. Dave would write scriptures about trusting God on hospital facemasks and send them to our room helping to cheer us. It was amazing how God used these two people, also fighting for life, to encourage us.

On Steve's fifth day in the hospital, the doctors told us his bone marrow would arrive that evening. The day was long, and Steve grew quiet and pensive. I was extremely nervous but excited, thinking about the miracle of it all. It was clear that Steve and I were not sharing the same emotions. We had to trust God individually since we were not able to lean on each other. In my journal I wrote, "In the dark God is there. In the emptiness He is there, and I am convinced in the future He is there too."

✂ LIVING MATTERS ✂

- Oswald Chambers says, "Every man is made to reach out beyond his grasp. It is God who draws me, and my relationship to Him in the first place is a personal one, not an intellectual one."
- I am convinced that God is real even when I can't see him. Pushing through the fear of the unknown future, I was challenged to believe He was there, even in the dark, empty space beyond my grasp. Every dependence here on earth is temporary, but dependence on God is eternal.
- There may come a circumstance in life that will give you an opportunity to reach out beyond your grasp and find God's hand.

✍ 7 ✎

SISTER'S SACRIFICE

The greatest love is shown when a person lays down his life for his friends. John 15:13

In the early hours of August 10, Sister Mary Ann lay on the operating table. Her mind traveled over the past days. She was about to donate her bone marrow—a perfect match for someone she would never know. Sister Mary Ann was willing to lay down her life in this way, for a stranger. She thought, *Because I am a nun I will never give birth. This is God's plan to allow me to give life in another way.*

Fred Hutchinson Cancer Center told her it was standard policy to withhold information about the donor or the recipients who were involved until one year after the transplant. She only knew the person who would receive her bone marrow was a forty-five-year-old man who lived 3,000 miles west of Boston.

The procedure used to collect the bone marrow (called bone marrow harvesting) takes place in an operating room, usually under a general anesthesia. It involves little risk and minimal discomfort. Before Mary Ann agreed to donate her bone marrow, the doctors explained some of the risk factors and discomfort she might experience.

While she was under anesthesia, a needle would be inserted into the cavity of the rear hipbone where a large quantity of bone marrow is located. The bone marrow—a thick, red liquid—would be extracted with a needle and syringe. Several skin punctures on each hip and multiple bone punctures would be required to extract the required amount of bone marrow. Usually one to two quarts of marrow and blood is harvested. While this sounds like a lot, it really represents only 2 percent of a person's bone marrow, which the body replaces in four weeks. When the anesthesia wears off, Mary Ann would feel some discomfort at the harvest site. The pain is said to be similar to that associated with a hard fall on the ice. She would be discharged after an overnight stay.

Mary Ann thought just momentarily about all she was told, but she knew this was an opportunity to give one man his only chance to live.

The doctors donned their masks, and asked, "Are you ready, Sister?"

She nodded.

The anesthesiologist placed the mask over her face. She was soon asleep. The doctor began harvesting the bone marrow that represented life for Steve.

As Sister Mary Ann was making this sacrifice, there was a whole order of sisters, even internationally, who were praying for the donor who would be receiving this gift of life. How awesome to see how long and entwining the tendrils of God's love truly are.

Two quarts of bone marrow taken from Sister Mary Ann were frozen and stored at a temperature between minus 80 and minus 196 degrees Centigrade. The doctors placed the precious life-giving substance into a cooler and gave it to the courier who was waiting outside the operating room. It was then flown to Seattle and taken directly to Fred Hutchinson Cancer Center.

Several hours later, 9:30 P.M. Western Pacific Time, Steve's new immune system came down the hall in a Styrofoam cooler. When they lifted the three very full IV bags out of the container, I looked through the plastic at Steve and saw tears rolling down his face. There were no words to explain the emotion that welled up inside our hearts. I was overwhelmed with excitement and awestruck with God's amazing grace. This moment will be framed in my mind forever.

The courier handed me a card, jolting me back to the reality of my surroundings. The card arrived with the bone marrow and read, "Dear Friend, I want you to know that you are in my thoughts and prayers, and will be in the days and weeks ahead. My gift to you is a gift of love. Your Donor."

We were allowed to ask generic questions about Steve's donor. Debbie, the courier, told us her name was Mary Ann. She was thirty-seven years old, single, never married, and never had children. This was significant, because male patients receiving marrow from a female donor who has had two or more viable pregnancies also are more likely to develop acute graft-versus-host disease. In graft-versus-host disease, the donor's bone marrow does not recognize the body it has entered, perceiving it as foreign, assaulting the recipient's organs and tissues. This increases the patient's susceptibility to infection and can be life threatening. God supplied a tailor-made miracle, specific in every detail. The card that came with Steve's new bone marrow revealed the person behind his only chance for life. I experienced a bond with a woman I'd never met. Together we were willing life to Steve.

The transplant process began immediately. The bone marrow was infused into Steve's body through the Hickman catheter, like the countless transfusions he had already received. As the nurse connected the two IV lines, she commented, "This is a lot of bone marrow. This donor is going to feel like she's been kicked by a mule. She will be doing what we call the 'Hutch Shuffle.'" I breathed a sigh of gratitude for Mary Ann's sacrifice.

We watched the red fluid run it's course, through the tubing, into Steve's body. As the bone marrow reached the point of entry, an inexpressible emotion welled up in my throat, a mixture of tears and laughter. Our God is an awesome God.

Knowing the process would take about eight hours, I had arranged to have a bed put into Steve's room. Even though we were separated by the plastic sheet, I was near him through the night.

As the bone marrow was being infused, Steve began experiencing fever, chills, and chest pains. He vomited at least every hour during the night. The doctors told us this would happen. Our joy was mixed with suffering. Neither Steve nor I slept much. I could only lie there and listen as my friend suffered until sunrise. At 5:00 A.M. the transplant was completed. Now the days and weeks of waiting began.

God was becoming very large in our eyes. There was no way to contain God; he could no longer fit into the box of our imagination. He would come when He wanted and in whatever way He wanted. It became our mission to look for the ways God would come each day.

✍ LIVING MATTERS ✍

- Oswald Chambers said, "God's Spirit alters the atmosphere of our way of looking at things, and things begin to be possible which never were possible before."
- This unexpected crisis, the circumstance of illness and my need of a larger-than-life God, gave me a changed view of Him. God had altered forever the way I looked for Him. God no longer had limitations.
- Is God limited in your life? Don't limit Him! He may come in a person, a phone call, a scripture, a card, or a song.

❧ 8 ❧

SMALL BEGINNING

Do not despise the small beginning, for the eyes of the Lord rejoice to see the work begin. Zachariah 4:10

The weeks following the transplant were the most critical. Chemotherapy and radiation had destroyed Steve's bone marrow, crippling his immune system, and giving him no defense against infections. In addition, the donor marrow perceived Steve's body as a foreign body to be destroyed.

The doctors had only one way to fight the bone marrow's attack-medication. Drugs were used to suppress the donor bone marrow, allowing a gradual graft. Blood samples were taken daily to measure the progress of the graft and to monitor organ function.

In addition to being the smallest component of the white blood cell, lymphocytes are the backbone of the immune system. The white cell count within the blood indicates whether the bone marrow is engrafting. Nurses at the Hutch nicknamed this part of the white cell "Poly." Steve needed five-hundred Polys before doctors would release him as an outpatient. It would be several weeks before we would know if the bone marrow would accept or reject Steve's body as its new home. In Psalm 139: 13–14, the Psalmist says, "You knit me together in my mother's womb. I am fearfully and wonderfully made. Your works are wonderful, I know that full well." This truth and our body's complexities were never as real to me as during the days following the transplant.

The morning following the transplant, I got off the elevator and I headed straight for the nurses station. The attendant handed me a slip of paper with Steve's morning blood count. The Poly count was at zero. Walking into Steve's room, I taped our first Poly count on a large calendar that hung on the wall. This became my morning ritual.

Two weeks passed. On day seventeen, I became very anxious about the counts. Outside Steve's room that morning I asked the doctor, "What happens if the graft doesn't take?"

The doctor said Steve would receive other medications to simulate his new system, "But," he added, "I'm not concerned at this point."

Oh really, I thought, How could it be too soon to worry? People all around us are dying because their Poly count was low. I knew that every patient on this floor was hoping and praying for the five-hundred Poly count. And for some, there were no Poly counts, I struggled to keep my mind on God and his promises of peace. Be still my heart.

About 9:00 that evening, as I was saying goodnight to Steve, he pulled the sheet up over his head and began to desperately cry. I felt helpless. I pressed my hands onto the plastic. I wanted to hold Steve in my arms and comfort him. The thin wall of protective plastic that separated us seemed miles thick. Through tears I spoke his name, "Steve, Steve, I love you. I love you."

Steve said, "I am so lonely. I feel so isolated. Even though I can see you, I can't touch you. This is harder than I ever thought it would be." We wept together. It broke my heart to think of leaving him that night.

It was my habit to call Steve's dad before leaving the hospital each night. Tearing myself from Steve, I made the call and then headed for the apartment. Approaching the second block of my lonely walk home, I saw my father-in-law in the shadows of the streetlights. He was striding toward me. When I reached him, I burst into tears and he put his arm around me. As we walked side by side, I leaned into his shoulder and told him what happened with Steve that night.

We cried together, then he began to call out to God. He asked God to touch this man we both loved.

Getting ready the next morning, I heard a knock on the bathroom door. I responded, but there was no reply. I opened the door. Steve's dad, Quent, stood silently with the phone in his hand. Unable to speak, he handed me the receiver.

I said, "Hello?"

There was no sound.

Then I heard my husband, who had not phoned since entering his isolation behind the plastic curtain. With a broken voice he said, "I got twenty Polys."

I broke into shouts of joy and tears. I hugged Quent, who was still silent, but was smiling through watery eyes. Grabbing my jacket and shoving my feet into my shoes, I ran the four blocks to the center. I jumped into the elevator at the first floor reception room and began punching the second floor button. It seemed the elevator climbed in slow motion. The doors were half-open when I leaped

63

off. Rounding the corner, I couldn't keep from running. I headed directly to the nurses station, trying not to run into anyone.

Before I could get to the nurses station, the attendant said, "Did you hear? Poly said hello."

"I heard, I heard!" Taking the slip from her hand, I ran to Steve's room. We pressed our hands together through the plastic. Looking at the paper, there was finally a number on it. "Twenty Polys!" I hurried over to tape it up on my calendar. It was as if we had won the lottery. We were jubilant as we counted twenty Polys down and four-hundred-eighty to go. My heart told me all was well. This sweet memory will be with me forever.

Zechariah 4:10 says, "Do not despise this small beginning, for the eyes of the Lord rejoice to see the work begin."

I started down the hall to share the good news with my new friends Dave and Linda. Linda knew exactly how I felt and rejoiced with me. They were a shining example of how God can use people. He encouraged us through their lives. Linda shared her knowledge, explaining medical terms, telling me what to expect from day to day. My prayer is that someday, we too, will be used by God to support others.

More encouragement came through an article written by Dave Dravecky, a major league baseball pitcher who lost his pitching arm to cancer. In his article, "When You Can't Come Back," Dave wrote, "I have always had an answer for everything, but now I know there aren't always answers." He went on to describe how his focus shifted from his own needs to the needs of others. He wrote eloquently of the many wonderful people he met and how much he learned from them all. Through the cancer, he had learned so much about life. He said, "To have missed this, now that would have been a real tragedy."

While I would never choose to have cancer, I agree with Dave Dravecky, that we would have missed the opportunity to see God's hand in so many ways had we not endured the closeness of death.

One afternoon our pastor, Steve Schell, came to visit and pray with us. It really lifted my husband's spirit. Before Pastor Steve left, he said, "I believe your story will be told." Turning to me he said, "Gwen, I think you are going to be the one to tell it."

Although his words were thought provoking at the time, I knew my heart was not ready to do anything without Steve, nor did I want to. I thought, *What a story we will have to tell when we get home.*

✍ LIVING MATTERS ✍

- Oswald Chambers says, "We have seen what we are not, and what God wants us to be, but are we willing to have the vision 'battered to shape and use' by God?"
- My father would often encourage me to see the lesson and life application by asking the simple question, "Did you learn anything?" If I answered, "Yes," then he would reply, "Tell them what you have learned." The education acquired from a crisis not only can be character building, but will be useful to touch another life, if God is allowed to use it.
- Give God the difficult circumstances, and he will batter them into shape and use them.

✎ 9 ✎

SUSTAINED

Cast your cares on the Lord and He will sustain you; He will never let the righteous fall. Psalm 55:22

Death surrounded us at the Hutch. People, we had come to know and love, were dying daily. Yet, miraculously, God seemed to protect and sustain Steve. Every day the bone marrow produced more and more Polys. Steve no longer received red cell and platelet transfusions to strengthen his body. His new bone marrow was doing what it was designed to do, produce the cells to live. This was an occurrence we would never take for granted again.

The doctors said we could go home in two weeks. Home meant our Seattle apartment. We still would have sixty days of outpatient care before doctors would let Steve return to our home in Milton. Though excited, I began feeling apprehensive about the many duties I would assume in caring for Steve. A week before Steve's release, I panicked, doubting I could properly care for my husband: I worried about his fragile immune system and the possibility of my infecting him.

Even though I attended classes for caregivers, learned how to use the IV pumps and needles, and learned how to administer the many medications he would need, I was terrified. As the week progressed, I felt more and more afraid. Three days before Steve's discharge day, I pressed my hands on the plastic and pleaded, "Steve, will you learn how to do this IV pump? Will you help me with the budget?"

Steve looked at me in anger and disbelief. Though still very weak, his voice rose, "Gwen! No, I can't help. You are going to have to do it yourself!"

Shocked, I burned inside. I was angry at Steve's reaction, and I was angry with myself because I was so immature. Amazingly, Steve's words and actions helped me more than he ever knew. I thought, *I will do this. I can learn without Steve's help.*

On September 9, exactly forty days since Steve walked across the threshold, the plastic wall that separated us was finally lifted. As I crossed the forbidden opening, excitement filled my heart. Weeks had passed since Steve and I put our arms around each other, now he was only four feet away with no barriers separating us. As I walked toward him, our eyes fixed on each other, tears began to stream down our cheeks, and we began to smile. Our arms reached out and we embraced for a long time. Neither one of us wanted to let go. Four hours later, we walked out of the hospital, and on to the next leg of our one-hundred-day journey.

Though together again, there was an uneasiness between us that hadn't been there before. We had changed. Having just come through such a difficult battle, we were both emotionally raw. Steve was frail and unsure of himself. I was sensitive and afraid. The constant barrage of drugs made him irritable, touchy, intense, easily overwhelmed, and confused. Diabetes, another side effect of the drugs, required daily insulin shots. Some days Steve's hands would tremble, making it too dangerous to inject himself. He was forced to rely upon my assistance. Being easily upset, Steve lacked confidence in my ability to meet his medical needs.

Recovery is a long process. When Steve was especially despondent and unsure of himself, I told him the same things I told our friends. I was the stronger one, providing reassurance. We had switched supportive roles.

The next sixty days passed with ups and downs. Our life consisted of daily outpatient clinic visits and attending to Steve's many medical needs. At times I tired of being nurse and caregiver and just wanted to go back to the way things were. One morning in particular, as I lay in bed not wanting to get up, Steve crawled in next to me and whispered in my ear. "Where are you Gwen? What's going on?"

At first I said, "Nothing, I don't want to talk about it." Then, enjoying Steve's attention, I began to share my self-pity. "I love you, Steve, but I feel so unimportant and useless. I'm nothing more than a caregiver, cook, chauffeur, and cleaning lady. I want to share life with you. I want something more of our life together."

Steve held me and listened quietly. Then he responded, "Well, Gwen, I know this hasn't been easy for you, but you have to take responsibility for your thoughts. You're either listening to lies or the truth magnified."

I knew he was right. It was such a blessing to have my friend, my husband, speak to my needs again in his kind and gentle way. I thanked God, realizing how much I had missed these precious moments. I attended a support group designed for the special needs of caregivers. Here, I was able to vent my feelings and gain a sense of comradery. Still it did not replace my need to share with my husband and gain his understanding. It helped also to have Dave and Linda, who knew what we were going through.

Dave and Linda lived in the same apartment building. We saw each other in the elevators, at the clinic, and passing in the halls. Linda became my mentor, continually encouraging me. Even though she and Dave had struggled with leukemia for over eight years, she still maintained her faith in God, lending enormous courage to others. She was a great role model, demonstrating that sometimes our strength has to be peeled away so we can truly rely on God's strength.

I referred to Linda as my best friend from Connecticut; she called me her best friend from Seattle. When the doctors released Dave and they were ready to fly home, I was sad for me and glad for her. We planned to meet again the following year at our one year checkup. Steve and I said our good-byes. We hugged them and waved as they drove away to the airport.

As we watched them drive away, I realized the importance of each day and making them count. I was learning to slow down and embrace the "nows" of life that I once would have missed or avoided, I embraced our remaining nine days as another opportunity to see God in new ways. Five days before we were released from Fred Hutchinson, Steve was given his last bone marrow biopsy. We celebrated when the results came back negative—no more leukemia!

✎ LIVING MATTERS ✑

- Joni Eareckson Tada says in her book, *When God Weeps*, that He screens the trials that come to each of us—Allowing only those that accomplish his good plan. She goes on to say that every trial in a Christian's life is ordained from eternity past, custom-made for that believers eternal good, even when it doesn't seem like it. Nothing happens by accident . . . not even tragedy.

- It is hard to agree with the above statement until we look back at a time of suffering. Then we see things with more clarity. Though we are not always willing vessels, God can use a tragedy to accomplish His good plan. We discover truth about ourselves, but more importantly about Him.

- What truth about yourself and God have you learned through a difficult time?

September 1990—Camping in the San Juan Islands.

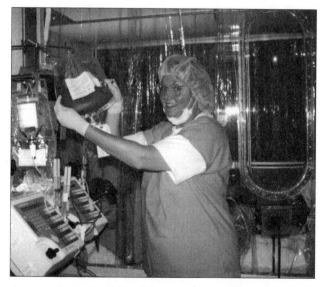

August 1993—Fred Hutchinson nurse holding the donor bone marrow, about to begin the transplant process.

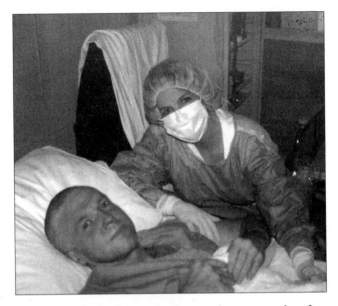

Steve and I behind the plastic curtain, two weeks after transplant, waiting for the donor bone marrow to graft.

September 1993—Steve and I in the out-patient clinic, 40 days after transplant.

April 1994—Eighteen days before Steve's death. Kneeling left to right: Julie, Danny, Jake. Sitting: Steve

October 1994—Sister Mary Ann (Steve's donor) and my favorite Nun.

Mother's Day 1999—Embracing life today. Danny, Me, and Jake.

10

STORM SHELTER

I would hurry to my place of shelter, far from the tempest and storm. Psalm 55:8

On November 18, 1993, Steve was behind the wheel of our car heading down I-5 toward home. I sat beside him barely able to contain my excitement. We had won our fight against leukemia and we were going home to Milton—together. God's hand orchestrated an elaborate miracle. He sent bone marrow from almost 3,000 miles away. Bone marrow from a stranger who was perfectly matched down to the blood type. God sent finances, food, friends, family, church support, and, most of all, his fellowship. Steve's daily visits to the clinic had evolved to weekly visits. Now we were ready to begin the next step, helping Steve rebuild his immune system and his strength.

Steve took exit 142B off I-5 heading toward Milton. As we turned the corner onto our cul-de-sac, with our video camera running, I asked Steve to slow down so I could record every second.

There was a sign hanging on the garage that read, "Welcome home, Steve and Gweny, Praise the Lord!" I felt tugs of love as I recognized my sister Sally's writing. She was so thoughtful. As the garage door lifted, to reveal all that was familiar, we were filled with elation. Walking through the house, we soaked in the sight and smell of everything— our furniture, our kitchen, our bedroom, and our yard. We loved our home, it was not just a dwelling; it was our refuge and our haven. And it seemed so large after living in a one-bedroom apartment.

As we started to unpack, the doorbell rang. Friends delivered a complete turkey dinner. We all embraced; the phone began to ring. Family and well-wishers called to make sure we arrived home safely. We were loved. *Thank you, Lord, for bringing us home healthy. Thank you for bringing us so much support and love.*

Steve could not attend church because there were too many people, especially children—the primary virus carriers. So I attended church without Steve. As I entered the lobby of Northwest Church, my first Sunday back home, my eyes fell on a sign posted on the bulletin board which read, "Steve Bagne is Home!!!" It was awesome. When I told him about the sign and the many well-wishes, he smiled, eyes brimming with tears.

He loved hearing about the wonderful outpouring of love for him, but he still missed the fellowship. Working with our situation, a small, "healthy" group of friends came to our house once a month. They sang, prayed, and ministered the Word to my husband. Our friends understood our need to limit visits and willingly submitted to my interviews about any colds or viruses they may have. Antibacterial soap was cautiously used before contact was made with Steve.

One month later we were faced with the Christmas holiday. This was an especially difficult time. Our sons and their families came over, and we opened gifts as we had every year. Steve could not join us for the large family gathering at my brother's house. All my brothers and sisters and the many small children made it impossible for him to attend. We didn't want to leave Steve alone, but he insisted. "It's all right, Gwen. We have next year. Go and enjoy yourselves."

Right! I thought, as if that were possible without him. As we loaded up the car and drove away, I felt tears well up inside as I left him sitting in his chair.

New Year's Day, 1994, brought with it new hope, and life took on a routine. January 30, Super Bowl Sunday, Steve was feeling good, and we enjoyed the day. Since it was still too soon for Steve to join large groups, I went without Steve to our End of the Month Club at Rick and Darcy Battershell's house. The club was a support group we started to help people manage their finances using God's plan. The meetings reinforced God's financial principles and helped people stay on course. Rick and Darcy stepped in as leaders to help when Steve got sick.

Rick and Darcy were well qualified to lead our financial mission. They were certified with Larry Burkett's organization, Christian Financial Concepts. Rick was our accountant and financial advisor, but most importantly he was a friend during the time Steve was in the Hutch. Rick and Darcy were two of the many who walked with us and supported us during our fight against leukemia.

The meeting was a blessing. It was good to be with friends who helped us through our darkest valley. Rick asked, "Gwen, what made this last year a great one?"

I shared how God brought us through a time of suffering and taught us many wonderful things about Himself and His people. "To sum it up: my faith is greater, God is bigger, priorities are clearer, friends are dearer, family is closer, Jesus is sweeter. A verse of an old hymn comes to mind, 'He washed my eyes with tears that I might see.'"

I never tire of telling this story, proclaiming God's power, sharing the sweetness of knowing him, his fellowship, and his sufferings. So it was, as Pastor Steve had said, I would be the one telling the story.

March 1, 1994, Steve took back the budget responsibilities. I rejoiced. Life was returning to a normal pattern. Steve was in charge, and I loved it! Now I could go back to my pattern of doing lunch and visiting with friends. A great weight lifted off my shoulders: I was thrilled about our future.

Easter weekend the kids came for dinner and our three-year-old grandson, Derek (I call him Sweet Boy), spent the night. It was his first overnighter in a year. We read stories, ate ice cream cones, and stayed up late. What a fun night!

After Easter Steve went in for his weekly doctor visit. He was pleasantly surprised when the doctor took him off all medications and told him he need not come back until next month. Dr. Rudolph was amazed at Steve's progress.

The following week we drove down to visit Steve's parents in the small coastal town of Ocean Shores. This was our first get-a-way since Steve's illness. We enjoyed the weather, the ocean, and, especially, Steve's parents. We had all been through so much together. Now we enjoyed each other in a new way.

We joined Steve's dad at church. It was the first time in a year that Steve and I attended church together. When the pastor asked Steve to share his testimony with the congregation, Steve told everyone all God had done to help him live and how God worked through the many people we met during the ordeal. Our hearts were moved.

The next morning, backing out of the driveway, Steve suddenly stopped and looked at his mom and dad standing in front of the garage. He said, "They are getting older; they won't always be there." I glanced at Steve, took my camera, leaned out the window, and snapped a picture of them. Steve put the car in gear again. We headed for home.

✎ LIVING MATTERS ✐

- Verdell Davis wrote a prayer in her grief: "God, you take the broken pieces and infuse them with new life, bind them up with your grace and give us strength for our weakness, courage for our fears and joy for our failings. Make us strong in our broken places and do in us what we cannot do for ourselves."
- Webster's defines the word *broken* as shattered, ruined, and useless. God has taken something shattered and ruined in my life, like a broken marriage, an addiction, and facing a fear, and made it useful. As God infuses the broken pieces, they can then bring life and strength to others. All this is accomplished only in his hands. It's a God job!
- What broken pieces in your life can God infuse and use?

❧ 11 ❧

SENTENCE OF DEATH

We do not want you to be uninformed, brothers, about the hardships we suffered. We were under great pressure, far beyond our ability to endure, so that we despaired even of life. Indeed, in our hearts we felt the sentence of death.
2 Corinthians 1:8–9

We were looking forward to a camping trip we'd planned with Rick and Darcy. We would caravan to North Bend, a small logging town, thirty minutes southeast of Milton. We were thrilled. Life was beginning to feel good again

Monday, Steve loaded the camper on the truck. The rest of the week he worked diligently, preparing it for the road. Steve had already purchased a book for the trip, Dr. James Dobson's book *When God Doesn't Make Sense.*

On Friday afternoon, I stepped inside the camper to see how Steve was doing with the preparations. He was sitting on the floor. Looking up at me, he said, "I have a headache. I feel so weak."

My heart sank. I thought, *Oh no, this can't be happening, not now.* I felt a bit of anger at having to wait some more. But then I told myself it was just a camping trip, not my life. "It's okay if we put this trip off," I told Steve. "Why don't you come in and rest awhile?"

Steve dragged himself off the floor and followed me inside the house. He took a Tylenol for his headache and lay on the couch.

"You know, Steve," I said. "It's important to take extra precautions right now. We will have plenty of time to go on camping trips. Why don't we cancel this one." Steve was disappointed, but told me to call Rick and Darcy to tell them the change in plans.

Overnight the headache became more painful. I called Dr. Rudolph.

He prescribed pain pills, but said, "If Steve's headache isn't gone in twenty-four hours, bring him to the hospital." Steve grimaced when I told him. Even though he could not eat and didn't have strength to get out of bed, he dreaded going back to the hospital.

Sunday morning Steve could barely move. "Steve, we have to go in," I said. "You don't have mature bone marrow. Let's go."

As I helped Steve dress, he kept saying, "Lord, have mercy on me. Lord, have mercy on me." Steve was so weak that he staggered into the wall as he left the bedroom. Reeling from the impact, he said, "Help me, Lord. Give me strength."

I helped Steve into the car, put the seat all the way back, and placed a pillow under his head. Steve laid his hat over his eyes to block the sun. He didn't utter a single word on our trip from Milton to the Virginia Mason Hospital.

Steve needed my help to walk from the car to the emergency room. When we stepped through the emergency room door, Steve, always the caretaker, tried to pull his medical card out of his wallet. He lost his balance and almost fell. I helped him to the nearest chair and told the nurse he needed to lie down, now. I said, "Steve, it's okay. I can take care of this."

The nurses helped him onto a hospital gurney and wheeled him down the hall into the examining room while I filled out paperwork. Steve's headache was so intense he asked the nurses to turn off the lights. When I completed the paper work and returned to Steve's room, it was dark and quiet. I left him alone so he could rest and I could make a few calls to let people know where we were.

I called our families and friends. No one was home at Steve's parents, so I planned to call later. I told myself, and those I called, there was no cause for concern. This was just a precaution. Eighty-five percent of all bone marrow patients were readmitted for one reason or another.

I sat beside Steve's gurney while doctors performed a spinal tap and other tests. The doctors decided to admit him so they could observe him, and find out what was causing the headache. Attendants administered more pain medication to make him comfortable, which made him sleep. As Steve slept, I wandered out to the hall, stepping into the room periodically to see how he was doing. Steve did not say much, he only asked that I leave the lights off.

Hours passed. I took my pocket Bible from my purse, and it fell open to 1 Timothy 5, the chapter giving advice to widows. I read the chapter, but before I could reflect on the meaning and implications a nurse approached me saying, "There's a phone call for you."

I walked to the visitor's lounge and picked up the phone. It was Steve's dad. I told him the hospital was admitting Steve and that I would call when I had more news. Being optimistic, I added, "The doctors know it's an infection, but don't know what kind. I'm sure they'll figure it out soon and we'll be home in a couple of days. Keep praying. I love you."

I returned just as the attendants were wheeling Steve to his hospital room. I followed as they wheeled his gurney into the elevator. He had a vacant look in his eyes, and remained silent. When we reached room 425, I watched the attendants skillfully maneuver the gurney into his room. They lined the gurney up with the hospital bed and transferred Steve from the gurney into the bed. A nurse brought a rollaway bed into the room for me to sleep on. After settling in, I made a few phone calls to update family and friends.

The next day, hospital staff still could not find the reason for Steve's headache. When Dr. Rudolph arrived in the afternoon, Steve seemed to recognize him and smiled weakly. The doctor began asking him questions. "Who is the President of the United States? Do you know where you are? Do you know what day it is? Steve, glancing in my direction, seemed unsure of himself, but tried to answer. As I witnessed his confusion, a cold chill went up my spine. I was numb with fear. Steve would say nothing unless he was asked a question. Dr. Rudolph ordered a CAT Scan.

Later that same day the CAT scan revealed an infection in Steve's brain. I thought, *The infection caused Steve to have headaches and confusion. It's the reason Steve had difficulty answering simple questions. As soon as the infection is cleared, we can go home.* I didn't allow myself to register the increasing danger.

That afternoon, Pastor Steve and Pastor Les came to the hospital to see us. After they left, I stood beside the bed looking at Steve, when I noticed a blister on his arm. Immediately I called the nurse. Everyone went into high gear. They swabbed the area where the blister was, took a culture, and sent it out for tests. Within an hour the results came back. Steve had chicken pox.

Danny, my oldest son, came in to see us on his way home from work. As he entered the room, he greeted his dad then talked with me a while.

When Danny got up to leave, Steve spoke his first complete thought in four days. "I love you, Danny."

Danny responded, "I love you too, Dad," and hesitated a moment before he left the room.

Later, Steve's parents and sister arrived. I could see from their bewildered looks that they felt as helpless as I did. Looking for some kind of support, I asked Steve, "Do you know what's happening?" He looked at me blankly.

That evening, a decision was made to move Steve to the infectious disease floor. His new room overlooked Lake Union. As they transferred Steve from the gurney to the bed, he struggled to lean forward, attempting to see out the window. Always loving a view of the water, he lay there not saying a word, gazing out at the lake.

Steve's parents left and I felt sure we'd also be leaving soon. It seemed to me a simple matter of clearing up the infection. Steve would be on the road to complete health and all would be well.

✒ Living Matters ✑

- James 4:13–16 says, "Now listen, you who say, 'Today or tomorrow we will go to this or that city'. . .why, you do not even know what will happen tomorrow."
- Steve's last prayer, "Lord, have mercy on me. Lord, give me strength," is something I have reflected on many times. Calling upon the Lord to the very last is the thought that invades my mind—not calling to me or his dad or his pastor, but to God who is our ever-present help in time of need.
- Who will you and I call out to in our final moments?

∽ 12 ∾

Sorrow's Storm

Even though I walk through the valley of the shadow of death, I will fear no evil, for you are with me. Psalm 23:4

Our friends, Jerry and Sue Clark, came to see us. Sue walked in the room and immediately began teasing Steve, as was her usual custom. A smile of recognition crept across Steve's face, but he said nothing. Jerry remained outside the room, emotionally overwhelmed. It was too much for Jerry to see his friend suffering again. After a brief visit, Sue said good-bye to Steve. The three of us walked to the elevator. We chatted some, and then hugged our good-bye's. I promised to keep them posted.

I walked back into the room, shocked to see Steve sitting in a chair near the window. I couldn't believe my eyes. "Steve," I questioned anxiously, "What are you doing up?" As I walked closer Steve looked up at me; I could see he had fallen. His right eye and upper lip were swollen. "Steve, you fell down.

You fell and hurt yourself." I kept repeating myself over and over, half-disbelieving as I helped him back into bed.

Steve's lip was bleeding, but he turned away and would not let me examine it. He took a little sip of water through a straw, looked at me, then violently arched his back and began to make a horrible groaning noise.

Running out into the hallway, I began to scream, "Help! I need help!"

It was like everyone was moving in slow motion.

I screamed again. "Move it! Move it! Move it. Let's go!"

Steve was convulsing.

I began crying, "I left him alone. I left him alone and he fell down. He fell down."

A nurse grabbed me and sat me on a chair. "Listen," she said. "This was not your fault. It is not your job to watch him; it's our job."

I sat dazed, watching as my precious husband was still convulsing on the bed. I thought he was having a heart attack, but he was having seizures. Drugs did not stop the seizures. Because Steve was thrashing about, the nurses strapped his hands and legs down to the bed. I was living a nightmare.

It seemed like an eternity as I watched medical people running in and out of the room. Feeling guilty for leaving Steve in the room alone, I asked myself over and over again, *Why did I walk Sue and Jerry to the elevator? If I had stayed here, this wouldn't have happened.*

A nurse came in to sit beside Steve's bed during the night. My friend and lover continued to convulse and moan. Lying on the cot next to Steve's bed, I listened as he moaned and moaned. Thinking my heart would break, groans began to come up out of me. Never hurting so much in my entire life as I did at that moment, I cried without any thought of who might be there. I wailed from my gut, crying out to God, "Please, please, help us. Oh God, I can't do this."

I pressed my face into the pillow, then caught my breath when I faintly heard someone's voice. I stopped crying and listened. *Did I hear someone praying?* I sat up and moved toward the railing of Steve's bed. In disbelief, I asked the nurse, "Are you praying?"

Looking directly at me, she stated firmly, "I am, and I believe we serve an able God who can do anything. Nothing is too hard for him."

I was stunned and could only stare at her. She prayed as if she were alone, and I knew in this desperate moment that God had sent her for me. God had assigned a Christian nurse to sit and pray for my husband the whole night. Exhausted, I lay down on the bed and listened to her, finally resting.

Friends MiMi and Richie Drexler arrived within the hour. It was late, but there they were. MiMi led me to the waiting room with a pillow and blanket. Richie stayed with Steve. I fell asleep on the little couch in the waiting room, but soon awoke with a start and ran to Steve's room. Like a recurring nightmare, there was Steve, still moaning and pulling at the straps. I called to Steve over and over again, "Steve, can you hear me?"

There was no response—just moaning.

At three o'clock in the morning, I walked back to the waiting room and lay down again. There was nothing to do but wait. I could not even pray. Then in the background I could hear the thud of heavy footsteps coming down the hall toward the waiting room. They were heavy, stomping footsteps. They seemed especially loud in the silence of the hospital hallway.

The nurse assigned to my husband rounded the corner into the waiting room. Holding an open Bible in her hands, she walked directly toward my friend and me. She began to speak lovingly, but firmly, about the God of Abraham. "God told me to tell you, He has everything in His hands and knows right where you are. You are to trust Him." Shoving the large black opened Bible onto my lap, she told me to read. She pointed to Isaiah 50:10, "Let him who walks in the dark, who has no light, trust in the name of the Lord and rely on his God." Turning on her heels, she headed back to her post next to Steve's bed.

As her footsteps faded away, my friend and I looked at each other in amazement. God had just walked down the hall, invading the thick darkness of fear, to encourage me.

I laid my head down on the pillow, and sleep finally came. When I awoke a few hours later, I walked to Steve's room. He, too, had quieted. As more support arrived, MiMi and Richie went home, the others gathered around Steve's bed. I sat unable to speak a word. There was nothing in me. But God sent fresh troops to pray. As this group left, family began to arrive.

The infectious disease specialist came to explain what was happening. Looking straight into my eyes, Dr. Winterbauer said, "Mrs. Bagne, we want to move Steve to the intensive care unit. He needs around-the-clock care, and we are not set up for that on this floor. We also want to put him on a ventilator, not because he can't breathe on his own, but so he won't have to work so hard. We are so sorry Steve fell and hurt himself. But we want you to know this fall did not cause his seizures. We were anticipating the seizures because of the pressure on his brain. The fall did not cause the seizures."

Once again, God was reassuring me with the doctor's words, but I was struck with the most unexplainable sense of urgency and fear. It came over me and was unlike anything I had felt until that point. I tried to dismiss this obviously misplaced feeling. "The peace that passes understanding" washed over the sense of foreboding. I would later realize such peace comes and covers when we are least able to comprehend what is happening.

The attendants came to transport Steve to intensive care. He was in a coma and covered with chicken pox. Four days had passed since the headache brought us back to the hospital. I looked at my husband wired with tubes and monitors. *Is this really happening?*

People came to the hospital. The waiting room quickly filled. God's people were praying, I couldn't.

When Steve was no longer contagious, the doctors ordered another CAT scan and prepared to take him out of intensive care. They were checking for brain damage.

Friends and family gathered to pray while we waited for the results.

Pastor Les told me to talk to Steve and to give him a love call. He said I was the only one who could do this. "Tell him what you want," Les said.

I went into Steve's room and leaned toward his ear. I half-pleaded, half-encouraged saying, "Steve, please, I want to go home with you. Please wake up and take me home. I want to go home to Milton. Don't go Steve. I need you." I lay my head next to his and cried, not wanting to accept what was taking place.

The next morning, the neurologist called us into a private waiting room to give us the results of the CAT scan. "Mrs. Bagne, I am so sorry, but Steve's brain stem has been damaged."

"What does that mean?" I asked. "Can you fix it?"

Looking me in the eyes, he spoke slowly. "No, this can not be repaired." He went on to explain that the brain stem is the message center. Among other things, it tells the body to breathe.

I stared at him, hating him for his words.

"Steve will never be able to breathe on his own."

I just couldn't believe that this was happening. *What in the world was God doing?* In shock I sat there trying to take in the words. "Does this mean it's over?"

"I am afraid so," the doctor said.

Steve was in a coma and dying, but many still believed God would work a miracle. Darcy sent a note that read, "Don't look at your faith, but look at God's faithfulness." This message encouraged me to take a deep breath, relax, and let God and others carry me for a while. I had no faith for this; I was just "there."

Steve's parents had rented an apartment for me across the street from the emergency room. When everyone left, my Mom and I went to the apartment. We fell into our beds that night exhausted. It was 11:00 P.M., April 25.

At 1:00 A.M. on Tuesday, April 26, I sat up in bed, wide-awake. I felt an urgency to see Steve. Throwing on my clothes without waking my mother, I ran across the street to Steve's unit. I rang the nurse's station for permission to enter the intensive care unit. The door swung open and I rushed to Steve's room. They had tied Steve down because he was thrashing about.

Realizing I had not been alone with Steve in so long, I crawled up onto the bed, getting as close to him as possible. "Steve, Steve," I cried into his ear. "Steve, what am I going to do? No one can help me."

He began to move about more as I spoke to him, as if to reach for me.

I told him, "I don't want you to go, but if you go I will be all right."

I lay beside Steve weeping and talking to him for several hours.

Growing quiet, he never moved again.

As I left, walking past the window between ICU and the hallway, I saw my mother. She led me into the waiting room and told me to lie down on the small couch. Mom rubbed my feet until I fell asleep.

Later that morning, Dr. Winterbauer met with Steve's dad and me. He said, "Steve will not survive the day. You can turn off the machines now or you can wait. He may survive ten minutes, or he may survive twelve hours. It's your decision."

My decision. Taking a deep breath, I leaned back into the chair. *How do I get my heart to hear what he just told me?*

We had a family meeting and prayed together, or I should say, they prayed. I just sat there and listened. Expressing my heart, I shared that I did not want to stop anything prematurely. Steve had fought a good fight and was in no pain. I felt strongly that he should be allowed to finish his course. Our son, Jake, who had brought his portable keyboard, began playing "Amazing Grace" softly in the background. We gathered around the bed to let Steve go.

The day was surreal. Steve's body was slowly failing, but his strong heart beat on. As his body began to shut down, he turned cold. I continued to pile blankets on him.

I momentarily stepped out of Steve's room when my brother, Tom, came in about 9:00 P.M. "You better come now, Gweny. The heart monitor is beginning to drop." We gathered around his bed. Jake, Danny, and Julie, Danny's wife, were standing beside me. I put my face into Steve's neck and whispered, "I love you, Steve. I love you." In the background a cassette tape was softly playing "He is the God that healeth thee."

The doctor leaned toward me and spoke the words, "He's gone."

My response was, "He's gone?" Looking at the heart monitor, the line was flat. The ventilator was still pushing air into Steve's lungs, but he was gone.

There was weeping all around me as I stood beside my husband. Not wanting anyone to touch or comfort me, I told the nurses, "Take all the tubes off, then come and get me. I'll wait out in the hall." I turned and walked out.

Sitting outside the doorway, I heard laughter and conversation up and down the hallways. People were acting as if nothing had happened. I wanted to shout, "Quiet please! Steve Bagne just died. Can't we have some silence and a little respect?"

The doctor approached and sat across from me. With a hushed voice he spoke, "Gwen, we will never know how Steve got this infection. It could have been in the bone marrow or harbored in his own body. Chicken pox is a virus, so it could have been in the elevator. We will just never know."

I walked to the waiting room as family and friends gathered around me. About half an hour later a nurse walked up and handed me Steve's wedding ring. It was as if she had handed me my heart. She said, "He's ready for you now." Moving slowly, my heart racing in anticipation, I entered his room. I could see the husband that I had loved wasn't there, only his lifeless body lying under a white sheet.

Sitting in a chair next to the bed where my husband's body lay, I was so alone. The machines were turned off. The silence was deafening. There was no comfort, because Steve was gone. Looking at Steve and then up at the ceiling, I said, "It's you and me again, Lord. I am a widow." I remembered 1 Timothy 5, the chapter about widows I read when we arrived nine days earlier. I heard in my heart the words, *"Trust me."* I left the room as my sons went in. So it went until everyone saw Steve.

I was speaking on the telephone to my brother, Jack. He was crying. I wasn't. I sat numbly listening to Jack, when a nurse approached.

"Where do you want the remains to be sent?" She asked. Remains? Did she say remains? I was stunned. How could she speak of my beloved in such a clinical manner?

She must have observed my shock because she nervously, continued on, telling me of her mother's death. She told me Steve would always be with me, watching over me. I wanted to tell her to shut-up, that Steve was in heaven and would not be watching over me. Was this supposed to comfort me? I soon realized this was only the beginning of many well-intended, but comfortless comments I would hear.

It was midnight as I left Steve, the man I loved, lying in the hospital morgue. Family and friends surrounded me as we walked across the street to the apartment. I felt dazed as I put one foot in front of the other. When we arrived at the apartment, everyone talked and ate, but it all seemed so bizarre. It was as if this were happening to someone else and I was an onlooker. I had experienced this sensation when Dr. Rudolph told us Steve might have leukemia. I had an emptiness in my heart and an ache in my stomach. Soon, everyone but my mom left. I lay down on the bed, sleep came like a savior.

When I woke up the next morning, I realized it hadn't been a nightmare after all. Steve was really dead. I bathed and dressed in auto-pilot mode, feeling my heart had stopped beating too. Facing the mirror, I thought, *Is that me? What am I doing, and what am I going to do?* I finished packing my clothes. My Mom and I checked out of the apartment.

97

Though my family and friends were concerned, I wanted to drive home by myself. Walking to the garage where Steve and I had parked the car, I got in behind the wheel. I looked at the passenger seat where Steve's pillow and hat still lay, proof that he had been there. *Was Steve really gone?*

I drove out of the parking garage onto the freeway. It was a beautiful spring day; the sun was shining, and the birds were singing. I was aware of how strange the loveliness of the day seemed against the darkness of my soul. *Only nine days ago I drove into Seattle a wife. Now I was driving home to Milton a widow.*

Steering the car into the driveway, I saw Steve's beloved camper. I pushed the button on the garage door opener. When it lifted, I saw Steve's tool belt lying on the floor. There was a tug on my heart. It felt like he could appear at any moment. Going into the empty house, I collapsed into a living room chair. Never anticipating coming home alone, I sat unfeeling in silent exhaustion.

✍ LIVING MATTERS ✍

- Verdell Davis said, "I have begged God for answers and thanked him for the trust He sent instead. I have felt His peace on the mountaintop and sensed His wisdom in the valley.

- There are times when life seems to be a riddle that has no solution. What do we do then? When we have pleaded with the God of heaven for help and the illness ends in death or the marriage ends in divorce, do we still trust God? Yes! This is where our doubt turns to faith. He will never let us go.

- In Hebrews 13:5 (Amplified), "For He (God) Himself has said, I will not in any way fail you, nor give you up, nor leave you without support. [I will] not, [I will] not, [I will] not, in any degree, leave you helpless, nor forsake, nor let [you] down, [relax my hold on you]—Assuredly not!"

- When all you can do is hang on, know God will always hang on to you.

~ 13 ~

SEE YOU IN THE MORNING

I hope to see you soon, and we will talk face to face.
3 John 13

J ust choose the one you want," the funeral director said.
Steve's dad, my mom, my son Jake, and I walked between the rows of caskets. Steve and I had decided we did not want the other to spend a lot of money on the trappings of death. It was possible to spend a sizeable amount of money on a funeral, but our earlier decision helped me put things into perspective. We narrowed the choices down to two. Jake made the final choice. I was so glad my son was with me. We then had to go through the same thing at the cemetery.

"Just choose the plot you want," the woman in the office said.

Never having picked a plot, we wandered through the green cemetery lawn looking at what was available, overwhelmed with the many choices. Jake, again, chose a place near a group of trees. "It reminds me of camping," he said. "Dad would have liked it, and it will be easy to find."

Driving home in silence, I felt nothing, and yet I had just picked a burial plot for my husband. I walked into our house and down the hall to our bedroom. I looked through Steve's clothing, handling everything with care. Choosing a white shirt, his favorite tweed jacket, and gray slacks, I laid them on the bed. I sat down, trying to relieve the gnawing ache in the pit of my stomach. My eyes were frozen on the wardrobe Steve would wear. I stayed in the bedroom until the church called to ask who would sing what songs and who would speak. Dazed, I made the many decisions for my husband's funeral. Somehow it all came together.

Two days later I was stroking Steve's hair as I stood beside the casket. Steve wore the clothes I'd chosen, and he looked as though he might open his eyes at any moment. I knew Jesus could raise people from the dead, but would Steve want to come back? If he knew the pain I was in, wouldn't he want to come back? Part of me wanted him back, yet the other part of me knew that God had called him home. My heart asked, *How do you leave the viewing room and go on living? Why should I go on living?*

At the funeral, hundreds of people came "to pay their respects," as they say. There were a lot of tears, yet I couldn't cry. The service was beautiful and honored my husband. Dave Kleier, Steve's best friend, who was also the best man at our wedding, spoke along with Steve's boss. My brothers and sister-in-law sang some wonderful gospel songs, as did my dear friend Sue. Many people shared special memories. Pastor Les read letters from my sons, Danny and Jake.

Dad,

When I think of you I think about when you sat Jake and me down and asked us for Mom's hand in marriage. How did I know saying yes meant I would be receiving such a great dad? I think about when you'd wake up while camping. The first thing you'd do is open the door and take a deep breath of that fresh camping air that surrounded us. I'm thankful for you, loving and taking such good care of us all these years. For being a great husband to my mom and a great dad to Jake and me and instilling so many great qualities in me, that I might be able to put the same qualities into my family. I am thankful we were able to give you a namesake, Derek Steven, while you were here to know and enjoy. Dad, I will always think about you and miss you.

    With all my love,
    Your son Danny

Pastor Les, overcome with emotion, stopped for a moment. Clearing his throat, he asked us to excuse him, then he went on to Jake's letter.

There is a lot I could say about my dad and what he taught through our time together, but there's so much. I know how much my dad loved me. [You] see, every time we hugged one another he would say with a tear in his eye, "I love you, Jacob!" Then I could hear him gulp. [You] see, I could tell by the look in his eye. My dad was a sincere man. He was a faithful and loving man to my mother, but more important, he was faithful to God— especially in prayer. Every morning before [Dad went to] work I could hear him faithfully in prayer. That was one of the many things that impressed me about my dad. One last thing that will stick with me forever is a note from Dad in my mom and dad's budget book:

"A leap of faith without a net makes us want to hedge
our bet.
The waters never part until our feet get wet.
There's a higher place to go, beyond belief.
Where we reach the next plateau, beyond belief."
I hope I can be as great a man as my dad, cause to me he
was and still is the greatest.
Just for you, your son,
Jacob P. Bagne, April 30, 1994

My sons' testimonies were the only words that drew
emotion from me. They were a witness of how one man's
life can impact another, especially when that man's life is
given to God.

After the service, I went home, leaving my husband at
the church in the casket. We delayed the graveside service
until Monday. The city code and labor union regulations
prohibited burials after 11:00AM on Saturdays. I thought, *I
must endure another good-bye in two days. Will this torture
ever end?*

Somehow, the two days passed, and I found myself sitting in front of the casket again. People at the gravesite
ceremony told me Steve was in a better place and that he
wasn't in any pain. I smiled and thanked them. But I think
they were trying to make themselves feel better. They sure
weren't comforting me. I did not want to hear any words. I
only wanted to feel the pain. Why did I feel so irritable?

I was glad when my father-in-law brought me home.
And glad when everyone left and I could be alone with
my thoughts. I needed some time and space. Steve was in
the cemetery, and I was in our bedroom. I lay down on the
bed listening to the beat of my own heart. *Can this be real?*

In the days that followed I numbly took up the business of living. Everyone had gone home, and Steve was never coming home again. How was it possible to feel so much nothing? I wanted to get out of the house and go somewhere. But where? Calling a friend, I packed a bag, filled the gas tank, and headed over Snoqualmie Pass to Wapato, Washington. It is a small town in eastern Washington where my friend Sherrie and her husband, Bob, live on a 2,500-acre mint farm. Their beautiful home sat in the middle of mint fields. The sun beat upon lush green plants causing the aroma of mint to fill the air. As I sat beside the swimming pool, there was a peace that surrounded me. I felt comforted. I wrote in my journal: "May 21, three weeks and five days since Steve left me and this world. I'm at Sherrie's alone. As I watched a movie, 'A Man Called Peter' that morning, Peter Marshall made the statement, "One door slams, so God may guide you through another. We find God in life's unthinkable experiences. Former glory is not enough for anyone. Future glory." What's ahead?

A comfort came into my heart. *I think I am going be all right.* I had no idea that it was the calm before the storm.

◜ LIVING MATTERS ◝

- Joyce Landorf says, "I was wandering in the wilderness of grief, utterly devastated. I tried to find my way out—without letting anyone know I was lost—but the map books I read were filled with sticky-sweet poems and unreal directions."
- Like Joyce Landorf, I too felt I was a wanderer in the wilderness of grief. Christians do not grieve like those who have no hope, *but*

we still grieve. Until I experienced the trauma of a severe loss, I had assumed it would be different for a Christian. Grief is said to be a wound to the living and it takes time for a serious wound to heal. But there is good news, God does take us *through* and beyond the valley so we can embrace life again.

- If you have you been surprised by the intense pain of loss, know that you are not alone and that it is a normal response to losing a loved one.

✒ 14 ✒

SINCERELY, STEVE

Husbands love your wives as Christ loved the church and gave himself for it. Ephesians 6:25

Within a few weeks of Steve's death, just before the pangs of grief were upon me, I had more business to face—policies, pensions, and paperwork. I looked at the briefcase Steve prepared for me sitting on the dinning room table. Though I recognized its importance, I was not comfortable approaching the responsibility that was now mine alone. My coach and encourager was gone and I had to rely upon what he taught me. Unlocking the briefcase, my mind flashed upon the countless times I watched Steve diligently manage our finances. I fumbled with the lock and reluctantly lifted the lid. Suddenly my apprehension turned to panic as grief undermined any confidence I might ordinarily have had. Steve's neat penmanship and organization leaped from the contents. These were Steve's tools and I didn't feel equipped to use them. A lump filled my throat and I remembered my husband's words to me, "If you get scared, call Rick and Darcy, or my dad. They can help you."

Knowing I wasn't ready to face the financial issues alone, I closed the lid and made a call to Darcy. Sympathetic and willing to help, they came at the first opportunity. As I expected, we found everything in order—names, numbers, insurance information, a list of bills and schedule of payment days, including, characteristic of Steve's care, stamped and addressed envelopes. His attention to detail read like a love letter to me—"Gwen, I love you." My heart heaved a sigh of gratitude; my head questioned life without this caring man in my life.

The time and attention Steve invested in planning for us was such an act of love. Before Steve died, I viewed the budget as a boring hobby of my husbands; now I saw it for what it truly was—the blessing of provision by a man dedicated to God's principles. I recalled a friend of ours from Steve's work who unexpectedly passed away some years back. In the aftermath of his funeral, his widow asked us for our help in sorting out their financial affairs. This vulnerable woman had no knowledge of their finances and to compound matters, her late husband had nothing in order, not even an insurance policy. This lack of planning and preparation exacerbated the burden of our grief stricken friend. I thought, as I watched Rick sort easily through the paperwork, *That could have been me. I shuttered to think of it and thanked God for Steve's gift and provision.*

How grateful I was that Steve taught me the budgeting process. I was especially thankful for the kind and gentle way in which he took me step by step. I didn't realize it then, but his patient instruction over the past year equipped me to face what lay ahead. He cared for me in life, and now he was caring for me even after his death. As I considered my husbands provision, I felt emboldened to call upon God and face what lay ahead.

I scheduled an appointment with Rick the following morning. I'll never forget picking up that briefcase, getting into the car and heading to Rick's office. It felt like I was doing Steve's job, using his tools, yet peace filled my heart as I drove to see the man that my husband said I could trust. Nonetheless, I felt out of place without Steve beside me. I couldn't imagine how I could get accustomed to being on my own.

The following weeks I transferred our home, vehicles, camper, and other items into my name alone. I went from office to office, appointment to appointment in an apathetic motion. I had no feeling for the official business that was forcing me to face my widowhood. Nothing could ease the pain of realizing I must learn to face life without Steve, but the job was less complicated because the love of my life kept his house in order.

✒ LIVING MATTERS ✒
LEAVING GOOD NEWS BEHIND

Larry Burkett says, "Communicating about death neither hastens nor delays it; it only makes it easier for those left behind."

I know the whole subject of death and dying is not an easy or comfortable one to discuss, but if we don't take the time to talk and make sure we are prepared, we leave behind additional and unnecessary pain. Grief can and will bring with it an inability to make good decisions. It's so important for people to talk, write, and understand their finances and to have a plan such as a will or family trust.

DISCUSS AND WRITE DOWN

- The amount of life insurance, pension, and death benefits you have. After the death of a spouse, the costs of the funeral, medical bills, and immediate needs pour in. Having planned ahead is an incalculable comfort and relief to the family and loved ones left behind.
- Where are the policies? Whom should I call? Where are the phone numbers? Even the most routine duties become major trials during the shock of grief. It is a good idea to make a "Disaster File" that details all the information a surviving spouse will need to know.

KNOW

- How to keep a budget, how much you owe, and when it is due. Having been on a monthly budget, the surviving spouse is already accustomed to all the financial needs and responsibilities with which he or she is left. A budget also gives the surviving spouse a sense of security about family finances and confidence in the ability to readjust. The budget will change (i.e., an income decrease, lost medical coverage, etc.)
- How to balance your checkbook. This is part of being on a budget and a necessary discipline for both spouses.
- Have someone you trust to direct investment of monies. Well-meaning family members, friends, and outside influences will often try to advise you financially and will sometimes even ask you for loans. You need

someone you trust, who cares about you and has some knowledge of money matters, someone you can lean on through the rough transitions.

HAVE

- A will or family trust. Meeting with an attorney—while you are both alive—about your wishes concerning your children, business and investments is not a suggestion; it is a must! Going to court or having to hire an attorney after an untimely death will be a stress in the time of grief from which you should spare yourself.
- A Community Property Agreement. Those of us who are married and live in a community property state may think we need not make any additional arrangements. However, you will need this document as you make changes like selling automobiles, removing your spouse's name from the deed to your home and from bank accounts and many more tasks.

If you were to die today, what kind of a story would your family have to tell? Do the right thing, and love your family before you leave them.

Begin today to plan and provide so that you, too, can leave good news behind.

∽ 15 ∾

STEPPING STONES

Once more I will shake not only the heavens but also the earth. The words "once more," indicate the removing of what can be shaken, that is created things, so that which cannot be shaken may remain. Hebrews 12:26–27

Stepping out of the temporary numbness, afforded the newly widowed, I walked into a wall of pain. I thought my chest would literally burst from the ache inside my heart. I lay on my bed at night and cried for Steve, not for God. I couldn't trust God. God let this terrible thing happen to me when he could have stopped it. Now I was feeling grief's determined grip, and it held me tight.

When I had to return to the Fred Hutchinson Cancer Center on business, I saw Moreen, the social worker assigned to Steve and me. I broke into tears. She put her arms around me, and we walked into her office. As she handed me a tissue, I remembered only months before that Steve and I sat in the same chairs rejoicing as he was about to be released.

Moreen told me about grief and the stages I would endure. She said grief is like crossing a river and the journey is long. She explained that many people never leave the bank of the river, but remain there holding their grief. "No one can cross that river for you. They may walk with you, encourage, or stand on the other side and call, but it's your journey and there is life on the other side."

As she shared what this journey might look like, I sat silently, trying to absorb it all. I was thinking, *She's talking to me, a widow.* This information was not for anyone else, but for me. My silent prayer to God was, *Please don't let Moreen's words be true. Give me a shortcut.*

Though Moreen gave me an understanding of grief and told me what to expect, it wasn't enough. There was nothing in my background to prepare me for the incredible pain that took me hostage. The Bible says that sorrow endures for a night, but joy comes in the morning. For me, the nights were getting longer and it didn't look like morning would ever come.

There are many stones in this river called grief. Some are transitional, and some are to rest upon. I stepped off the bank of numbness and planted my foot firmly upon the stone of pain. I lingered there a long time. At times I could hardly breathe from the weight upon my chest. Then, unexpectedly, God invaded the great sorrow of my soul.

On a beautiful September day, Linda, my dear friend from Connecticut, called. "Gwen, are you sitting down?"

I caught my breath and asked, "Linda, is Dave okay?"

"Yes, thank you," she responded. "Do I ever have a story for you."

Linda told an amazing story about a woman she met at a dinner for bone marrow donors. The woman's name was Mary Ann. During dinner Mary Ann told Linda that she had donated her bone marrow to a man, but that he had died. All she knew was his name was Steve and he lived in Seattle. Amazed at the coincidence, Linda told Mary Ann that she also knew someone in Seattle named Steve who had leukemia and died. Linda asked Mary Ann, "What was Steve's wife's name?"

Mary Ann said, "Gwen."

Linda sat stunned with her mouth open.

Then Mary Ann said, "What? What!" They were astonished as they both realized they were talking about the same people. Linda was looking into the eyes of Steve's bone marrow donor.

God had again come into the darkness to let me know He was still there. Linda gave me Mary Ann's address—I sent a letter with pictures. Sister Mary Ann wrote back:

Dear Gwen,

It was so wonderful to hear from you and to receive the tape of Steve's memorial service and the article about the two of you. I was so grateful to God for meeting Linda at the dinner for bone marrow people and finally being able to hear more about you and Steve and about how Steve died.

My family and my religious community have prayed for Steve and for you and your family since I was matched with him. In the days before the transplant took place I felt like I was carrying his life in my body. When I was lying on the operating room table before the harvest began, I felt the Lord all around me and within me. It was a feeling of absolute peace and joy. I know now that I was supported not only by the prayers of my family and my sisters in community, but by all of you as well. Thank you for that. Donating bone marrow to Steve was a wonderful experience for me. Because I am a nun I will never give birth. Being able to donate bone marrow was, I believe, God's way of allowing me to give life in another way. My parents consider Steve and all of you part of us now because Steve shared my blood. It is doubly wonderful that we all share the same faith in and love for Jesus, too.

I was very touched by the memorial service for Steve. He must have been a very special man. You must really miss him. I am sorry that I never got a chance to meet him, but I look forward to meeting you.

Again, thank you for getting in touch and I look forward to seeing you.

Love, Sister Mary Ann

In October Steve's parents and I flew to Connecticut and spent two days with Sister Mary Ann, my favorite nun. Looking into the face of my husband's donor was an experience words cannot describe. It was one of the sweetest times of my life.

Shortly after returning home from meeting Mary Ann, I was struck with such a sense of loss. *Why did God go through all the trouble to heal Steve and then let chicken pox bring death? God, I want my old life and my husband back!*

During my grief and anguish, people tried to comfort me, saying, "At least he's in a better place. . . . At least he's not in any pain. . . . At least you're young. . . . You'll get over it."

Don't they know? I am the one in pain. I am the one not in a better place. I am never going to get over this! Any sentence that begins with "At least" is not a help to someone who is grieving. Now I know never to use those words in an attempt to comfort. Only the grieving person has permission to use them.

Some understood. They listened as I cried and told them how I hated God's plan. They let me embrace the sorrow and didn't try to take it from me. Most of the time words don't help when you're drowning in so much pain.

I left anger and leaped onto the stone of depression. I couldn't sleep or concentrate. I was forgetful and tired all the time. It seemed everyone had a life except me, and I wasn't even sure I wanted one. There wasn't a good reason for getting up in the morning, putting on makeup, or going to church. In my despair I thought, *All normal living seems absurd because, you see, life will never be normal again.*

I stepped back and forth among the stones of pain, anger, and depression. I grew tired of the journey, but I could never find my way back to the numbness that helped me through Steve's funeral. Then there was the stone of guilt.

All the what ifs and if onlys came flooding in: *What if we had gone to the hospital sooner? What if I gave Steve the infection? If only I'd been more patient with him.* These thoughts would torment me, but I was afraid to tell anyone for fear they would agree. The doctor's words, "We'll never know how Steve got chicken pox," helped quiet my anguished heart.

These words helped remove my guilt, but the bigger question of why loomed large in my mind as I cried, "God, I don't understand you anymore." Accusations, thick with sarcasm and childish whining permeated my conversations with God. Though my interaction with God was filled with tantrums, it was communication nonetheless. Joni Eareckson Tada, refers to this in her book *When God Weeps,* "*I am mad as a hornet, God, and I don't understand what you are doing one bit!*" Sounds like the dark side of trust but it's trust, nonetheless.

My pain was too great to carry alone, and having no where else to go for relief, I began to listen and lean on God again. One afternoon as I was praying, the phone rang as if on cue. The woman on the other end said, "Hi, my name is Marlen and I was asked to call you."

Marlen began to tell me about her journey through widowhood a few years earlier. I had finally found someone who could answer my questions. My first question was, "Will this pain in my heart ever go away?"

"Yes," she said, "joy will come back into your heart again."

I learned she recently remarried. At that moment I couldn't think about marrying anyone else. How could anyone take Steve's place? "Do you really love your new husband?"

"Yes," she responded.

Marlen gave me hope when all seemed hopeless. She listened to me, and when she spoke I believed her. God brought me comfort to begin the healing of my broken heart.

As I accepted and adjusted to life without Steve, I gained an interest in helping others. I knew there were men and women who were just beginning their own journeys through the river of grief. All the things, good and bad, that people had shared, I had written down. My experience gave me a new understanding of the grief process and I began sharing my journey with others. God always wants us to use what we have gained to reach back and take the hand of others and bring hope to them.

✒ LIVING MATTERS ✑
GOOD NEWS FOR THE GRIEVING

Matthew 5:4 says; "Blessed are those who mourn, for they will be comforted." Ecclesiastes 3:4 says, "There is a time for everything, and a season for every activity under heaven: a time to weep and a time to laugh, a time to mourn and a time to dance."

First, it is important to understand that we each have our own timetable, style, duration, and depth for grieving.

Second, after the death of someone you love, it is important to find people with whom you *feel safe in sharing your loss.*

Third, it is important to know most people who suffer a loss may experience one or more of the following:

- Tightness in the throat or heaviness in the chest
- Emptiness in the stomach and loss of appetite
- Guilt and/or anger with themselves, the deceased and others
- Restlessness and an inability to concentrate
- Disbelief—as though the loss isn't real, that it didn't actually happen
- A sense of the loved one's presence, like expecting the loved one to walk in the door at the usual time, hearing their voice, or seeing their face
- Aimlessness, forgetfulness, and leaving projects unfinished
- Difficulty sleeping and dreams of the loved one
- An intense preoccupation with the life of the deceased
- An assuming of mannerisms and traits of the loved one
- Intense anger at the loved one for leaving
- A desire to take care of other people who seem uncomfortable around them by politely not talking about their feelings of loss
- A need to talk, over and over, about the loved one

- Mood swings triggered by the slightest thing
- Unpredictable crying
- Turning toward alcohol, illegal drugs, or prescription drugs

Finally, find people who have experienced a similar loss and have recovered (i.e., support groups, material on grief, prayer, etc.), who can provide tools for the journey and an understanding about grief. No one should try to escape grief through drugs or alcohol. Such attempts at escape will only add problems, not take them away. The key is to mourn— do the grief work—only then will we be comforted.

↶ 16 ↷

Sorrow's Surprise

God, who comforts us in all our troubles, so that we can comfort those in any trouble with the comfort we ourselves have received from God. 2 Corinthians 1:4

Three years after Steve died, I was driving down West Valley Highway, on a beautiful August afternoon, heading toward the cemetery. As my mind drifted back, I thought about all the pain and anguish I had suffered. I thought about how God had carried, directed, guided, and used me. I now realized God healed me as He promised to heal the brokenhearted, but He healed me for the purpose of helping others as well.

Parking my car near Steve's grave, I looked around. I had planned to meet with a young widow named Sandy. Then I saw a woman get out of another vehicle parked on the other side of the graveyard. She waved and we walked toward each other. Someone had given Sandy my name and phone number as someone to talk to about her loss. Although we'd never met, we recognized each other immediately and embraced like old friends. We walked to a gravesite not too far from Steve's. We each took a corner of the blanket Sandy carried and spread it across her husband Martin's grave.

Sandy began pulling "memories" of Martin from a basket in her hands. She shared pictures of her marriage, her children, and the funeral. Her eyes filled with tears as she described how a police officer came to her door early in the morning six months ago. Martin died in a car accident. She described what life was like in the days following the shocking news. I began asking all the questions that I so wanted someone to ask me after my husband died. Questions that allowed her freedom to talk about her husband and her feelings.

As I listened I marveled at how similar Sandy's story was to mine and to the many other stories I'd heard over the past three years. At the same time I was amazed at the differences. Even though grief follows the same pattern, the circumstances of death and the circumstances of those left behind make every story unique. I'm always honored when I'm given the opportunity to share another's journey.

As Sandy and I sat in the graveyard where Steve and Martin were buried, I could see how God sent me to Sandy, just as he sent Marlen to me. Marlen reached out and took my hand, enabling me to reach out and take Sandy's hand. Now God was guiding and using me. I was the one listening to Sandy and giving hope to her hurting soul. As her heart is comforted, she will take the hand of another and lead them toward hope.

As Sandy and I walked from Martin's grave to Steve's, we were amazed at the picture. Two hearts came together this beautiful summer day to share life's pain and pleasures. Only God could have painted this masterpiece. The sting of death was like a strap that bound us to a shared knowledge of God's faithfulness. Once strangers, we now shared a life raft, wanting to thrive as well as survive. Without God's hand on our lives, we would never have met and shared this moment of comfort. We parted as if we had known each other forever. The day was a testimony to a faithful God. He had brought me through and beyond the storms so that I could touch another with the comfort I had received. This is what I like to call "a God thing."

✌ LIVING MATTERS ✍
CLUES FOR COMFORTING

Find those who can give insight and instruction so you can effectively minister to people who are in grief.

Realize we don't have to have all the answers. There are some questions that have no answer this side of heaven.

Listen, listen, and listen! The "laying on of ears" is more comforting than many words.

Understand that we cannot do the following for the grieving: We can't give them their loved one back. We can't take away their pain.

Here are things we can do for the grieving:
- Convey caring by touch
- Give permission to grieve
- Validate the loss and encourage the expression of feeling
- Remember with them
- Offer continuing support
- Provide printed material
- Link them with other grieving people (support groups or individuals)
- Pray with them

- Instead of saying, "If there is anything I can do, just call," take the initiative to call and to do whatever you think needs to be done—clean the house, cook a meal, baby-sit, run errands, answer phone calls, visit the cemetery or a support group with them
- Remember the most valuable thing we have to give is our presence
- Use the deceased person's name when talking about him or her
- Ask to hear about the loved one and to see pictures
- Share memories if you knew the one who has died
- When comforting, never begin a sentence with "At least." This does not validate the person's pain.
- Let touch convey caring (hand them a tissue and cry with them)

In Romans 12:15, we are told to mourn with those who mourn. The Greek word *mourn* in this passage literally means "to stoop over or to bend beside." When reaching out to help the grieving, remember to stoop down where they are living and not require them to step up to where you are living.

~ 17 ~

SERVING SINGLE

"For I know the plans I have for you," declares the Lord,
"plans to prosper you and not to harm you, plans to give
you hope and a future." Jeremiah 29:11

In this chapter I share three aspects of singleness I've discovered in my widowhood. Working with many widows over the years has revealed my experiences are common. I've listened to sad story after sad story, sorrow upon sorrow. Solomon's wise counsel in Proverbs 12:15 offers this: "The way of the fool seems right to him, but a wise man listens to advice." My prayer is that you will take Solomon's advice and guard your heart against the unecessary hazards that await those who have lost a mate.

Sorrow Upon Sorrow

In her book, *Learning to Walk Alone,* Ingrid Trobisch says, "The temptation to try and replace a beloved partner is strongest in the first year after experiencing loss."

One aspect of life I never wanted to face again was that of singleness. Yet about a year after Steve died I found myself struggling with intense loneliness. Nights and weekends were the worst times for me. Everyone seemed to have somewhere to go and someone to be with. As I cried out to God, all I could see was the long and lonely road ahead of me. I was alone. I belonged to no one.

I needed to get my bearings and wondered how other widows had dealt with this issue. I headed to the local Christian bookstore and made my way to the section labeled "Comfort." Selecting two books, one authored by Elisabeth Elliot and the other written by Catherine Marshall, I perused the table of contents looking for the I'm-remarried-and-living-happily-ever-after chapters. To my delight, both authors had remarried.

I had recklessly assumed that what I needed was another life partner. A few months later, while attending a local community college, I met a very handsome man. Enrolled in the same program, we had opportunity to spend a lot of time together. Our group of displaced workers and homemakers became another world for me, a place to escape my grief. Enjoying my new focus and potential future, I was open to the refreshment of life outside of the "grief zone."

As the weeks passed, this man and I shared long conversations. Our interaction brought back the comfortable and familiar memories of life with Steve and filled a void created by his death. I knowingly compromised one of my life's principles; the wisdom in men counseling men and women counseling women. Digressing from this truth, I allowed myself to develop an unhealthy emotional and physical attachment. I lost my ability to make good decisions and became blinded by my own desires. I foolishly believed my grief work was completed. I couldn't have been more wrong.

As the relationship progressed, I noticed small things that indicated his life was out of order. I wanted to ignore the warning signs and keep going. Proverbs 22:3 states clearly, "A prudent man sees danger and takes refuge, but the simple keep going and suffer for it." I enjoyed the momentary relief from my grief and sorrow. I found myself purposely keeping this part of my life private and avoiding any mention of him to those with whom I was normally transparent. But God in His love and faithfulness brought conviction to my heart and light to the situation. The path I was on now posted a "dead end" sign. The Bible admonishes us to "flee fornication" not just "stand and resist." I knew I had to turn around and run back to the safety of God and the people He placed in my life.

A timely dinner with friends provided an opportunity to share how I had become involved with this man. Concerned, my guests questioned the level of my involvement, and I shamefully admitted our kissing had stirred desires only marriage could satisfy. I had participated in what could have led to a serious transgression, indicating a moral weakness in my life. In addition, I turned a deaf ear to God and listened to my own reasoning. Because of my vulnerability, my friends discouraged me from further dating and suggested I spend time with my female and couple friends while God completed my healing.

Because of our long-standing relationship and their love for me, I was able to submit to them and their counsel. I won't pretend this was an easy task. I pouted for several weeks, angry with God but in reality angry with myself. The apostle Paul reminds us in Hebrews 12:11, "No discipline seems pleasant at the time, but painful. Later on, however, it produces a harvest of righteousness and peace for those who have been trained by it."

Single and Submitted

Following my dating blunder, I again focused on the business at hand: grief and the healing process. No matter how desperately I wanted to put it behind me and move on, there was no circumventing the necessary time and effort involved. I have often said, "To get through it, you must go through it." There are no shortcuts.

It took some time to forgive myself and break free of the shame and remorse I felt as a result of the choices I had made. In time and with a new view of the situation, I could clearly see where I strayed and why. Purposing to move forward, I considered how I would avoid this trap again.

Good boundaries are necessary to protect us from what can harm us. I had taken measures to protect myself against intruders and steer clear of danger. I double-locked my doors, installed floodlights, parked in well-lit areas, and screened my calls. Yet I had failed to invest the same care over my heart. "Above all else, guard your heart, for it is the wellspring of life," Proverb 4:23 warns.

I established boundaries for myself by determining what I would and would not allow in a social setting. I have five basic guidelines:

- First, potential suitors must be reputable Christians, preferably introduced by someone I know. Introductions via the Internet, personal ads, or dating services are not for me. In my opinion they pose unnecessary risk and produce mostly negative results.
- Second, I'm purposeful. If I don't see the ingredients of a solid friendship, I'm not interested. The Bible tells us to be cautious in friendship, and I warn singles to move slowly.

- Third, I exercise care initially by meeting in public places. Keep conversation appropriate and edifying, avoiding intimate levels of communication. Beware of flattery. Missing the affirming words of a mate causes a hunger for compliments. Proverbs 29:5 cautions, "Whoever flatters his neighbor is spreading a net for his feet."
- Fourth, I don't limit dates to one-on-one settings. Involvement in group activities will reveal much about a person. Introducing my new friend to established friends and family provides unbiased insight and a checkpoint for me.
- Fifth, all touch should be restrained to avoid defiling one another. I ask myself, *Where is this leading?* Instant gratification can rob us of our future and bring unwanted guilt to an otherwise potentially good relationship.

Until Steve's death, I had never lived alone or without a partner. It has been one of the most challenging events, but also one of the most rewarding. My adjustment to life as a single has developed slowly.

Pastor Steve gave me some great advice: "Gwen, find your purpose and become passionate about it, and you will intersect with the plan and person God has for you." Taking the time to discover who I am, even as a single, has allowed me to see my worth and value in God and to trust His plan for me. I want to encourage you to take time to learn about yourself. Allow God to reveal, heal, and fill the empty place in your heart. This is essential before you can truly give your heart to another. Don't settle for less than God's best for you.

Single and Satisfied

I can joyfully proclaim Paul's words in Philippians 4:12: "I know what it is to be in need, and I know what it is to have plenty. I have learned the secret of being content in any and every situation." The fact that I believe this still amazes me.

I have always considered marriage a good thing, and I hope that I can share in that partnership again. For now, however, I have made the choice to follow God in singleness, trusting His plan. My brother Jack once told me, "If you give yourself to God, you will love the things you used to hate and hate the things you used to love." God has brought fullness and purpose to my life as a single and given me opportunity. God will do the same for you.

✍ LIVING MATTERS ✍

When entering a new relationship, ask yourself
- Will this build me up or tear me down?
- Am I a stepping stone in this relationship or a stumbling block?
- Will this relationship draw me toward God or pull me away from him?
- Am I allowing God to provide, or am I attempting to meet my own needs?

❧ 18 ❧

SORROW'S SUPPLY

I will give you the treasures of darkness, riches stored in secret places, so that you may know that I am the Lord . . . who calls you by name. Isaiah 45:3

Someone told me four years ago I would find treasure in the pain. At that moment I had little hope that this would happen. But out of my grief, God gave me His heart for the hurting and tools to help. Today, I find great joy and satisfaction in three ministries birthed from my sorrow.

- *Leaving Good News Behind* is a nonprofit organization whose mission is to communicate, educate, and motivate others to prepare now, in practical ways, for an unexpected death and to provide comfort, guidance, and hope for those left behind. Steve's model has become my message. Each time I stand before a group and share my story about a briefcase that was filled with love and order, I see the treasure that was hidden in the darkness.
- *Young Widows Support Group* evolved as I shared with others how I found God in the midst of sorrow. Daily, God has brought people who need comfort and hope. I

consider it an honor to be part of mending broken lives. It's been said you can't give away what you don't own. Had I not allowed God to guide me through the storm, I would have nothing to give others. God gave me comfort. Now I have the joy of passing it on to those just beginning the journey through the valley of the shadows. As Marlen, Moreen, and others helped me, I can now help those who come after me. The young widows who sit in my living room sharing their sorrow are treasures I would never have looked for.

- This book, *Embracing Life Again*, is testimony to God's faithfulness and His healing power. The apostle Paul told the Corinthians, "You yourselves are our letters written on our hearts, known and read by everybody" (2 Cor. 3:2). I pray this book will allow God to use me as His epistle, to encourage your heart and help you in your journey with God.

The poem entitled "The Weaver," written by an unknown author, says it well:

My life is but a weaving
Between my Lord and me,
I cannot choose the colors
He worketh steadily.

Oftimes he weaveth sorrow,
And I in foolish pride
Forget he sees the upper
And I, the underside.

Not till the loom is silent
And the shuttles cease to fly
Shall God unroll the canvas
And explain the reasons why.

The dark threads are as needful
In the Weaver's skillful hand
As the threads of gold and silver
In the pattern he has planned.

∽ 19 ∾

EMBRACING LIFE AGAIN

I waited patiently and expectantly for the Lord; and He inclined to me and heard my cry. He drew me up out of a horrible pit ... and out of the miry clay ... and set my feet upon a rock, steadying my steps and establishing my goings. Psalm 40:1–2 AMP

Eight months after Steve died, Jake, my youngest son, moved in with a friend. The void was enormous. "Please Lord," I cried, "not an empty nest, on top of an empty bed and broken heart." It seemed like more than I could withstand. I could barely fathom the thought of adjusting to living alone. Could I live alone and be happy? Unthinkable! Many nights I entered my house saying, "Hello nobody. I'm home!" just to hear a voice. "It's just you and me, Lord," I would say as I sat alone in the living room.

We live in a world of change. Just as winter makes room for spring, so every purpose has its season. Solomon, the wisest man of all, tells us in Ecclesiastes 3:1, 5, "There is a time for everything and a season for every activity under heaven: a time to embrace and a time to refrain." Looking back over the past four years, I see God had a plan, though not of my choosing. I could not have imagined that I would say, "I love life!" and mean it.

I have since adapted to living alone. God has proven to be my faithful friend and, at times, my husband. Let me give you an example of how practical our husband-like God can be. The gutters on my home were over- flowing this winter. A recent storm had filled them with leaves and cedar branches, and my yard was in need of some maintenance. Complaining to the Lord that I needed help in this area, I reminded him I was without a husband. "This is a man's job," I whined, "and I am extremely tired of being needy."

Later that week Rick called and asked if he could come over and put some winter fertilizer on the yard. The next day while at Dave and Mary's, Dave asked, "How are your gutters?"

"Full and running over," I answered joyfully.

He said, "I'll be over in half an hour."

As I watched Rick apply the fertilizer on my lawn, and Dave clean the gutters, I reflected on the Lord's care; shown through these men.

God communicates in innumerable ways His care for me, never letting a week go by without revealing how intimately He is involved in my everyday life. He is a gap filler as well as a gap stander, and I only discovered these precious things about God when I needed Him in the simplest of ways. God always shows up!

My life is brimming with new people, places, and activities. I marvel at the life I now have that has come in great part because of the loss I have experienced.

It was in the stillness of those lonely days and sleepless nights that I found myself able to hear my own heart and God's voice. The years spent with Steve and the time I spent alone have been God's great investment in my life. Only the future and time will reveal the true return on these years. Yes, I have a future. Something wonderful has been planned for you too. We cannot grasp the exceeding great and precious things God has in store for those who belong to Him.

I have new dreams now and have embraced fully the life before me. He drew me up and out of the pit and set my feet firmly on a new path. God has a plan for me, and He has established where I am going. No longer do I look back and long for the former way of life. I see clearly the extent of God's ability to care for His children in the dark times and how absolutely His hand guides as the future unfolds before us.

I celebrate some joys today more fully, appreciating them with fresh eyes. No longer afraid of sorrow, I now allow it to teach me the lessons that can only be learned through loss. Knowing how quickly life can change and moments can be missed forever, I have purposed to listen, not only with my ears, but my heart as well.

Psalm 18:19 says, "He brought me out into a spacious place." With arms and heart wide open, I embrace life again and receive all that is before me. My life looks different today. I anticipate the adventures ahead. I don't know the future, but I know God holds it firmly in His hands.

ENDNOTES

Chapter 1: Storm Warnings
1. Oswald Chambers, *My Utmost for His Highest* (New York: Dodd, Mead and Company, 1935, 1967–1973), 254.

Chapter 2: Stormy Weather
1. Corrie ten Boom and Jamie Buckingham, *Tramp for the Lord* (Fort Washington, Pennsylvania, and Old Tappan, New Jersey: Christian Literature Crusade and Fleming H. Revell Company, 1974), 50.

Chapter 3: Something Strange
1. Chambers, *My Utmost for His Highest* (New York: Dodd, Mead and Co., 1935, 1967-1973), 285.

Chapter 4: Searching for Life
1. Wayne Watson, *"Walk in the Dark"* on *The Beautiful Place,* Nashville, Tennessee: Dayspring, 1993.

Chapter 5: Seeking the Savior
1. Chambers, *My Utmost for His Hightest* (New York: Dodd, Mead and Co., 1935, 1967-1973), 229.
2. Bob Cull, *"Only the Beginning"* on *Windborne* (Costa Mesa, California: Chalace Music, Maranatha Studio), 1979.
3. "The New Church Hymnal," song: *My Anchor Holds* (Lexicon music, Inc., 1976), 134.

Chapter 6: Separation
1. Chambers, *My Utmost for His Highest*, 357.

Chapter 7: Sacrifice
1. Chambers, *My Utmost for His Highest*, 286.

Chapter 8: Small Beginning
1. Dave Drevecky, "When You Can't Come Back," *Readers Digest*, July 1993.
2. Chambers, *My Utmost for His Highest*, 278.

Chapter 9: Sustained
1. Joni Eareckson Tada, *When God Weeps* (Grand Rapids, Michigan: Zondervan Publishing House, 1997), 56.

Chapter 10: Storm Shelter
1. Verdell Davis, *Let Me Grieve But Not Forever* (Dallas: Word Publishing, 1994), 21–22.
2. Webster's New World Dictionary of American Language, Cleveland and New York: World Publishing Co., 1957.

Chapter 12: Sorrow's Storm
1. Davis, *Let Me Grieve But Not Forever,* 145.

Chapter 13: See You in the Morning
1. *A Man Called Peter,* Twentieth Century-Fox Film Corporation, 1955, renewed 1979. (Peter Marshall quoted on video).
2. Joyce Landorf, *Mourning Song* (Old Tappan, New Jersey: Fleming H. Revell Company, 1974), 15.

Chapter 14: Sincerely, Steve
1. Gwen Bagne, *Leaving Good News Behind* (Federal Way, Washington: Northwest Church 1996), 7–9.

Chapter 15: Stepping Stones
1. Tada, *When God Weeps,* 152.
2. Gwen Bagne, *Crossing River Called Grief* (Federal Way, Washington: Northwest Church 1996), 7–8.

Chapter 16: Sorrow's Surprise
1. Bagne, *Crossing River Called Grief,* 9–10.

Chapter 17: Serving Single
1. Ingrid Trobisch, *Learning to Walk Alone* (Ann Arbor, Michigan: Servant Books, 1985), 90.

RECOMMENDED READING

Blue, Ron. *Mastering Your Money.* Nashville, Tennessee: Thomas Nelson Publishers, 1986.

Burkett, Larry. *Debt-Free Living.* Chicago: Moody Press, 1989.

Davis, Verdell. *Let Me Grieve But Not Forever.* Dallas: Word Publishing, 1994.

Landorf, Joyce. *Mourning Song.* Old Tappan, New Jersey: Fleming H. Revell Company, 1974.

Stewart, Susan K. "Bone Marrow Transplants." Highland Park, Illinois: BMT Newsletter. 1-800-654-1247 National Bone Marrow Program

Tada, Joni Eareckson. *When God Weeps.* Grand Rapids, Michigan: Zondervan Publishing House, 1997.

To order additional copies of

embracing **life** again

Finding God Faithful in the Midst of Loss

send $10.95 plus $3.95 shipping and handling to

Books, Etc.
PO Box 4888
Seattle, WA 98104

or have your credit card ready and call

(800) 917-BOOK